Block Captain's Handbook

Don E. Fletcher and Sarah Kaip

Edited by: Ted E. Lawson, Thomas N. Monson, David Sours

Advantage Source, Inc.
Medford, OR

Block Captain's Handbook

Advantage Source, Inc.
33 N. Central Ave.
Suite 219
Medford, OR 97501
(800) 867-0016
(541) 779-0016
Fax (541) 772-8239

Library of Congress Cataloging-in-Publication Data

Fletcher, Don E.
Block captain's handbook / Don E. Fletcher and Sarah Kaip ; edited by Ted E.
Lawson, Thomas N. Monson, David Sours.
p. cm.
ISBN 0-9743830-5-8
1. Crime prevention--United States--Citizen participation. 2. Neighborhood
watch programs--United States--Management. 3. Voluntarism--United States. I.
Kaip, Sarah. II. Title.

HV7936.C58F58 2004
364.4'3--dc22
2004017621

Advantage Source website: www.crimeprevent.com

ISBN 0-9743830-5-8

Contents

Introduction

Introduction

"Never doubt that a small group of thoughtful, committed citizens can change the world. Indeed, it is the only thing that ever has."

Margaret Mead

Community Watch is about groups of determined individuals engaged in the pursuit of common goals and dreams. Much of the good in this world occurs when *one person* decides to make a difference.

One cannot deny the incredible accomplishments of a championship football team? Or the achievements of a renowned symphony orchestra? Or the success of a group of citizens banding together to fund a library, fight drug abuse, or help the poor?

Just as undeniable, however, is the power of individual commitment. At Crime Prevention Resources, we believe that one person can make a difference. *The Block Captina's Handbook* will help you do just that. This *Handbook* will instruct you on what a Block Captain does within the context of your local Community or Neighborhood Watch Program. It will also help you discover the potential benefits to you, your neighbors, and the community.

What You'll Find in this Handbook

In these pages you'll learn some of the basics about Community Watch and how it works. You'll discover that each Community Watch Program is differs because of local priorities. Your program will depend on what individuals, families and neighborhoods in your community want to achieve. What are folks most concerned about where you live? Is it crime prevention? Child safety? Speeding drivers? Terrorist threats? Your Community Watch Program can address all of these issues.

The information applies to all types of communities. You can live in a village, a city, an unincorporated rural area, a marina district, in a multi-family housing unit, or on a university campus. Community Watch is effective in any of these situations. It also is effective in your workplace and your children's school. Business and school watch programs are increasingly common, and the Community Watch model can easily be adapted to these situations.

You'll also discover that an effective Community Watch Program depends on the cooperation of many people playing different roles. For example, someone needs to be the Program Coordinator. That's the person who gets people working together, talks up the Program to the Mayor or the Sheriff, helps the community identify potential funding sources, and manages the overall communication process. There's also a Steering Committee comprised of a cross-section of people from the community which helps to set priorities, build partnerships with businesses and civic organizations, and evaluate the Program's effectiveness.

The Block Captain plays a particularly vital role. We could even argue that it's the *most* important role, after the overall organizational structure is in place. That's because the Block Captain is on the front line, working to implement the program. The Block Captain is an effective gatekeeper for the exchange of information between the program leadership and his or her neighbors. The Block Captain also helps to plan block meetings so that they support overall program priorities.

The Block Captain's Handbook teaches the nuts and bolts of performing the necessary duties, should you decide to become a Block Captain. It provides the answers to frequently asked questions, such as: What does a Block Captain do? How does he or she do it? What do neighbors need to know? How do I get them to come to the meeting? How do we get a Community Watch block sign?

By the time you finish reading this handbook, you'll realize that it's not complicated being a Block Captain. It doesn't have to take a lot of time. But it does require forethought and attention to detail. Read this handbook and then discuss it with your Program Coordinator. He or she can answer any questions and help you get started.

WIIFM?

Ah, the question of the ages! WIIFM is shorthand for "What's in it for me?" Right now, we want to talk about the benefits *to you* of serving in your local Community Watch Program and why you should consider becoming a Block Captain. If that isn't clear in your mind, you won't be doing yourself or your Community Watch organization any favors by volunteering!

First of all, think of the benefits that you and your neighborhood will realize from having an effective Block Group. These include:

- a reduction in crime and the fear of crime
- improved community spirit
- social events to make the neighborhood more fun to live in
- better relationships with your neighbors

There are many other benefits. But you're probably thinking, "That's wonderful, but what will I personally gain by becoming a Block Captain?" That depends on your response to these questions:

- Do you want to make a positive difference in your community?
- Would you like to receive the esteem and respect of your neighbors and friends?
- Would you like to have neighbors you can go to in a time of need?
- Do you enjoy the feeling of accomplishment and of making things happen?

If you said yes to any of these questions, then ask yourself: Are you willing to give 5 to 10 hours per month over the next year in order to get these benefits? If the answer is yes, then you are definitely in the right place. Being a Block Captain in Community Watch is a great choice for you. Read on!

An Overview of Community Watch

An Overview of Community Watch

To be a successful Block Captain, you need to have a good background in the development of the Community Watch Program. How are you at history? That's what we're going to cover next—but don't worry, you won't have to remember any dates! We just think you'll find it interesting to know that the idea of Community Watch goes back a very long time.

History of Community Watch

As a Block Captain, you will talk to a wide variety of people in your neighborhood. Most people will have heard of Community Watch. If you ask them to define it, they'll probably say: "Isn't that the same thing as Neighborhood Watch?" They won't know the background. Giving them some historical perspective will demonstrate how the effectiveness of the program has progressed since its inception. The fact that Community Watch is based on earlier successful models should help inspire the confidence of the people you talk to.

Just about everybody has a story to tell about a friend who encountered and reported a crime in progress, thereby preventing further crimes. The idea of citizens being the eyes and ears of the police dates back nearly two centuries. It started with Sir Robert Peel, head of London's Constabulary (after whom London's famous "Bobbies" are named). In 1829, Sir Robert observed that the police are merely the paid representatives of the public, charged with doing full time what we all share as a basic civic responsibility—taking precautions to promote collective security and to limit criminal activity.

By the early 1970s, chiefs of police and sheriffs around the nation were frustrated by the increasing burglary rate across the United States. This trend was the result of several things. Society was becoming increasingly mobile and fast paced. Neighborhoods consisting of one-income families were rapidly changing. Two-income households were becoming the norm, leaving neighborhoods deserted during the day. Neighborliness seemed to be on the decline. People stopped being concerned about their neighbors' property and began keeping more to themselves. The unity and cohesion of the traditional neighborhood was gradually deteriorating.

Criminals recognized these trends and began to capitalize on them by quietly moving in and out of neighborhoods. Law enforcement agencies weren't able to keep up with the rise in burglaries. In 1972, the National Sheriff's Association developed a program to respond to this problem. It became the basis for today's Neighborhood Watch and Crime Watch programs. Numerous communities adopted and implemented Neighborhood Watch, sometimes with astounding success. The rate of burglaries decreased by as much as 75 percent in some areas. Watch programs were credited with reducing the rate of numerous other crimes as well.

What explains this phenomenal success? The answer is pretty obvious when you stop to think about it. People wanted to assume a more active role in making their communities safe. It was impractical to assign a law enforcement officer to each neighborhood, but it was very practical to utilize those who lived there. Residents within a neighborhood know who belongs there as well as what activities are suspicious. They can learn what's normal and what's not by becoming more observant. The most important reason Neighborhood Watch programs worked is because citizens began working *with* law enforcement instead of *relying on* them to combat crime in their community.

Naturally, these programs weren't perfect. There were obstacles to getting them started and to maintaining them. More than three decades have passed since the first programs began. They have evolved and have expanded to encompass more than just neighborhood concerns. Today, these community groups often start by addressing crime, but wind up addressing drug awareness, traffic safety, children's issues, personal safety, first aid, fire prevention, street repair, and city/county planning. More recently, they have become forums for neighbors and communities to discuss terrorism and disaster preparedness.

As these programs have evolved, practitioners have had to confront a variety of obstacles. For example, because Neighborhood Watch is often driven by law enforcement, such programs tend to be vulnerable to budget cuts, changing political priorities, and the periodic reassignment of officers. (In law enforcement, this is often called a "tour of duty.") Fundraising is a perennial challenge, and motivating newcomers to join and train as leaders is almost always an uphill battle.

The Development of Community Watch

In early 1990, Crime Prevention Resources began research to find the most enduring model of a community-driven program to promote public safety and citizen involvement. The principal findings of that study include the following:

- The most successful and enduring programs appear to have a significant civilian component in their organizing structure.
- The best models go beyond Neighborhood Watch. They are civilian-driven, with substantial consultation and coordination with police as well as other community organizations.
- The best models also have a broader mission than crime watch. The most successful programs have a citizen infrastructure that can address a wide variety of issues from health and safety to taxes and littering. They are also less vulnerable to philosophical or budget changes in law enforcement.

When Crime Prevention Resources published the first edition of the *Community Watch Administration Manual* in 1992, its emphasis was on community leadership. In publishing this manual, we built on the best practices we had observed during nearly three years of research. Among these were a strong Steering Committee comprised of a significant cross-section of the community (not just police), and a mission that went beyond crime watch.

Community Watch in the Age of Terrorism

These qualities have been emulated in many similar programs. The most recent development along these lines was precipitated by the rise of international terrorism. It's called Citizen Corps and it's a creation of the U.S. government that encourages individuals and groups of citizens to become more involved in their communities and to look for ways to prevent and thwart terrorism. Like Community Watch, Citizen Corps doesn't try to reinvent the wheel; it takes advantage of existing resources and offers an organizational structure and leadership model that is community based. It goes beyond crime watch and looks for ways in which community groups can collaborate on a variety of issues—disaster preparedness, in particular.

What Community Watch Is

You already have a pretty good idea of what Community Watch is all about, or you wouldn't be reading this handbook! However, just to make sure there's no confusion, here are the key features about Community Watch that you should be aware of.

Community Watch is a program comprised of individuals with a common goal of wanting a better place for their children, grandchildren and themselves. A place where they can grow up, go to work, raise families, and grow old. They want to create communities where they can live their lives comfortably and safely.

Like its counterpart programs—Neighborhood Watch and Crime Watch—Community Watch is concerned with the reduction and prevention of crime. But depending on the needs of its participants, Community Watch goes beyond crime prevention to address a wide array of other livability issues.

Community Watch trains citizens on topics ranging from home security and personal safety techniques to how to work more effectively with City Hall, how to prepare for a possible terrorist attack, and how to raise funds for a new playground. If it's something you and your neighbors need, your Community Watch infrastructure can help provide it.

Community Watch is a crime prevention program that:

1) Teaches citizens techniques to reduce being victimized.

2) Trains citizens on the importance of recognizing suspicious activities and how to report them.

3) Teaches participants how to make their homes more secure and properly identify their property.

4) Allows neighbors to get to know each other and their routines so that any out of place activity can be reported and investigated.

5) Creates a cohesive body of concerned citizens that can address other issues affecting the community—safety and health issues, terrorism, emergency preparedness, etc.

6) Encourages neighbors to collaborate with other organizations in the neighborhood and the wider community and to apply their new-found leadership skills to projects for the greater good.

7) Teaches leaders how to recruit, motivate, and train new leaders and thereby promote succession and vitality within the organization.

Similarities and Differences

Category	Traditional Neighborhood and Crime Watch Model	Community Watch Model
Organization	Blocks and neighborhoods reporting to police or sheriff's department	Blocks, neighborhoods, districts, reporting to the Steering Committee
Issues addressed	Crime Prevention, Homeland Security, Safety Issues (e.g., child safety)	Goes beyond crime prevention and safety to address priorities defined by the community
Decision-making	Law enforcement-driven	Civilian-driven through a Steering Committee
Coordinator	Almost always handled by a law enforcement representative: Police Chief, Sheriff, Crime Prevention Administrator, or Community Services Officer	Can be a law enforcement representative or a civilian
Leadership Development and Continuity	Often the Coordinator's position is a two-year tour of duty with little continuity between Coordinators	Strong emphasis on developing volunteers into leaders who can take on Coordinator or other duties in the organization
Funding	Comes mostly from the law enforcement budget with occasional donations from local businesses; often vulnerable when budgets are cut	Same sources, although greater civilian responsibility is assumed for finding alternatives.

What Community Watch Is Not

Just as you will need to answer questions about what Community Watch is, you will need to clear up confusion about what Community Watch is *not. It isn't*:

1)   A vigilante force working outside the normal procedures of law enforcement.

2)   A program designed for participants to take personal risks to prevent crime.

3)   A 100 percent guarantee that crime will not occur in your neighborhood.

4)   A panacea for all your neighborhood and community problems.

Benefits of Community Watch

A comprehensive Community Watch Program in your neighborhood (whether it is a high crime area or not) will have many rewards for you and your family, including:

- Feeling greater sense of security and well-being for your family and a greater sense of community. Community Watch puts the "neighbor" back into neighborhood. Community Watch also brings law enforcement and the community together as a team to reduce crime in your area.

- Reducing the risk of being a crime victim. The risk is reduced because participants are taught how to take preventive measures that substantially decrease the likelihood of becoming a crime victim. Law enforcement agencies report that not only does Community Watch reduce the risk of your home being burglarized, but the instances of other crimes such as vandalism, personal assault, and fraud also decrease.

- Being better prepared to respond to a suspicious activity. Part of the Community Watch Program is training on how to report suspicious activities in your neighborhood, what law enforcement officers need when a crime is being reported, and why.

- Having more greater access to information on criminal activity. Community Watch Programs are designed to keep participants informed of crime trends and patterns so that they will be better prepared to spot any crime activity and stop it.

- Receiving a Community Watch sign to post in your neighborhood. Criminals know that if a neighborhood has a Community Watch sign posted, that neighborhood is not an easy target. Community members have taken the necessary steps to deter crime in their neighborhood and that these precautions are being observed. Convicted burglars have reported avoiding neighborhoods that have Community Watch signs posted.

- Knowing your neighbors. Community Watch promotes getting to know your neighbors and their regular patterns so that each of you will be able to report any activity that doesn't fit with regular schedules. This means that when you're away, you can feel more secure about your property. This also instills more sense of community and puts the neighbor back into neighborhood.

- Reducing the fear of crime and making your neighborhood more livable. Community Watch increases the number of arrests and convictions by serving as a network for law enforcement and the community to communicate effectively about criminal activities.

- Allowing other issues of concern to the community as a whole to be addressed. Once crime has been addressed and the fear of crime has been reduced, Community Watch participants can move on to address other issues that concern the community as a whole—issues such as fire prevention, first aid, disaster preparedness, or whatever the group feels a need to address.

The Block Group

The Block Group

The Block Captain

The Block Captain is the heart and soul of the Community Watch Program. Block Captains bring the program closer to home for the participants on their block. They attend to much of the detail work that the Program Coordinator or District Coordinator is unable to do.

The Block Captain is the main communication link to the group of people on the block. He or she shares the concepts of Community Watch, promotes participation, and provides information and materials to participants. The Block Captain is responsible for organizing block meetings. He or she acts as a liaison to the District coordinator.

The Block Captain must live on the block he or she is representing. The duties can be shared between two Co-Captains. The responsibility of the Block Captain should be rotated every year to another individual on that block. This prevents burn-out and creates a greater involvement in the program. It also develops new leaders for the program.

Initiating a Block Group

The following is a summary of the process for starting a Community Watch Program on your block.

Talk to Your Neighbors

The first thing to do is to visit your neighbors door to door and explain that you are starting a Community Watch Program for your neighborhood. Inform them of the benefits of having such a program and ask them whether they might be interested. If they respond positively, tell them that you would appreciate their attendance at a brief exploratory meeting to gauge neighborhood interest.

Use the Citizen's Guide

Give them a copy of *The Citizen's Official Guide to Crime Prevention* and find out the best day of the week and time for a meeting. (For best results the meeting should be extremely brief—no more than half an hour—and held in a home on your block.) Ask them to read through *The Citizen's Guide* prior to the exploratory meeting. Inform them that you will get back to them about the date, time, and location. The *Citizen's Guide* is available from Advantage Source by calling 1-800-867-0016.

Coordinate Efforts With Local Law Enforcement

Telephone your local law enforcement agency to see if they have a Community Watch contact. It could be a community services officer, a crime prevention officer, the police chief, the sheriff or another department employee. Let him or her know what you are doing. Find out whether he or she would be available to do a crime prevention presentation if the neighbors are interested. Get some dates when the law enforcement representative might be available for such a meeting, and let him or her know you will call again after discussing it with the neighbors at your exploratory meeting.

Agree on a Meeting Date

After talking with your neighbors, you should be able to identify a date, time and location for the exploratory meeting. Fill out the meeting announcement flyer (see appendix), make copies of it, and distribute it to your neighbors.

Get Together to Talk About It

Hold the exploratory meeting. See page 35 of this handbook for a suggested agenda. Ask people to discuss briefly why they like the idea of starting a Block Group. Ask whether they would be interested in having a training session with the local law enforcement representative. Ask what other interests or issues they would like to address through such a group. Set a date, time, and location for the start-up meeting based on availability of the law enforcement representative. Distribute copies of the Family Data Sheet and the Crime Survey (see appendix) to each meeting attendee. Ask them to complete these before the next meeting. Also ask people to talk up the meeting and invite someone to attend it with them.

Follow Up Between Meetings

As time permits, collect the Family Data Sheet and Crime Survey so that you can get a head start on tabulating and evaluating the data. Such information will be helpful to the law enforcement representative in adapting his or her presentation to the group.

Promote the Start-Up Meeting

Between meetings, distribute flyers to remind people of the start-up meeting and to extend an invitation to those who didn't attend the exploratory meeting. Be sure to let everyone know if a law enforcement representative will be present. Many people are more responsive when they know that the police department is going to be present for the meeting.

Create a Block Map and...

Whether you collect the data sheets and surveys before the start-up meeting or at the meeting itself, use the information to complete a Block Map, Block Profile, and Telephone Tree. These forms are included at the end of this handbook. You'll want to distribute these to everyone at the start-up meeting or as soon as possible thereafter.

Hit the Ground Running!

Hold the start-up meeting using the agenda on page 35 as a guide. Please note that the agenda calls for some group business prior to the start of the crime prevention training session. Specifically, you will need to elect co-captains for the block. Ask your law enforcement representative to arrive about 20 to 30 minutes into the meeting. That should give you enough time to conduct your business without keeping him or her waiting.

Recruit Some Help

One of your objectives for the start-up meeting should be to get some volunteers to help with the next meeting, or with any special activities the group decides to pursue. Be ready with specific tasks, and be sure to ask them for their help!

Agendas for Exploratory and Start-Up Meetings

Block meetings are intended to educate Block Group participants about crime prevention and to provide training appropriate to the group's needs and interests. The meetings also provide the chief forum for transacting business on behalf of the group.

The initial meeting is exploratory in nature—its main purpose is to gauge initial interest and identify some preliminary goals. It should be kept under 30 minutes. You can also use it to distribute Crime Surveys and begin the process of collecting appropriate household data.

The start-up meeting includes a business agenda and an initial training session on crime prevention. If possible, this training session should be conducted by a local law enforcement representative. Many of the topics in this training session are covered in this handbook—the benefits of Community Watch, how to report suspicious activity, how to get a Community Watch sign for the neighborhood, etc. For your convenience, we have also included an outline that can serve as the basis for this training session. [See the Crime Prevention Presentation Outline on page 38.]

Here are some preparatory steps you can take in advance of the exploratory and start-up meetings. Make sure you know what sort of training your law enforcement representative is able to provide and when he or she is available. Have a sign-in sheet for each meeting. Have extra copies of the Family Data Sheet and Crime Survey available for people who didn't get them or forgot to bring them. Find out from your law enforcement representative what the rules are for putting up a block sign. Also find out how to start the home security survey process in case there are people who want to get started right away.

In addition to regular Block Group meetings, you should plan on at least one meeting a year with the District Coordinator or Program Coordinator. If possible, meetings with a participating law enforcement representative every six months would be preferable. Also, take advantage of any opportunity to meet with the group to conduct training. If members request it on a monthly basis and are attending regularly, find a way to ensure that the meeting takes place. This will keep enthusiasm high and benefit the program in the long run.

Positions of Leadership Within Community Watch

As a Block Captain, you need to be aware of how the Community Watch Program is organized. Ask your Program District Coordinator to sit down with you and explain the system to you. Following are generic job descriptions for typical positions within the Community Watch management structure.

Program Coordinator

The Program Coordinator is often the Crime Prevention Administrator with a local law enforcement agency, whose duties include not only Community Watch, but also Business Watch, block home programs, substance abuse prevention, citizen patrols, citizen's academy, etc.

Almost as often, the Program Coordinator will be a civilian. In either case, this person is required to oversee, coordinate, and manage all aspects of the Community Watch Program. It is important for the Program Coordinator to keep in touch with the District Coordinators and meet with them on a regular basis. (If your Community Watch Program is large enough that you are required to have District Coordinators, then it will be practically impossible to keep up with all that is occurring in your city without regular meetings between the Program

Coordinator and the District Coordinators.)

Responsibilities of the Program Coordinator include:

1.   Outlining a plan of action for the Community Watch Program.

2.   Implementing the plan of action.

3.   Writing job descriptions for the various positions to be filled as outlined in the plan of action.

4.   Keeping the Chief or Sheriff updated on the progress of all crime prevention programs.

5.   Acting as a liaison between the law enforcement department and the District Coordinators.

6.   Ensuring the smooth operation of all crime prevention programs and monitoring their progress. The Program Coordinator will be able to accomplish this because of his or her ability to know what is occurring throughout the city in relation to crime and crime prevention.

7.   Meeting with the District Coordinators on a regular basis.

8.   Gathering information that needs to be conveyed to the community through newsletters, Community Watch website (see the section on Communications for more details), or one page handouts (especially if the information is of an emergency nature, like crime hot spots in the city).

9.   Ensuring the distribution of newsletters and flyers through the District Coordinators or Block Captains. Ensuring that the Community Watch website is up to date.

10.   Designing and implementing training programs and arranging education programs (including those in schools) for the District Coordinators.

11.   Assisting District Coordinators in the implementation of their training programs for the Block Captains.

12.   In cities with a population of 100,000 or less, it may be the Program Coordinator's responsibility to recruit sworn officers to assist with training on the block level and make these individuals available to the District Coordinators. This type of training would be for blocks that request specific training or information on a subject like personal safety, drug enforcement, etc.. The officer would have specialized training or experience on that subject and would be willing to help out.

13.   Arranging an annual awards banquet.

14.   Working with the Steering Committee as a liaison representing the

law enforcement department.

Assistant Coordinator

Depending on the size of your community's program, the Program Coordinator may have an assistant with whom you interact from time to time. As with the other leaders in the management structure, this person is there to help you get results on your individual block. His or her specific job responsibilities are the same as for the Program Coordinator, but in a support capacity.

District Coordinator

The District Coordinator will be responsible for overseeing the operation of crime prevention programs in a specific area or territory of the city known as a "district."

A district is an area or territory, of the city, that is generally surrounded by boundaries such as rivers, freeways, specific streets, or mountains that divide the city proportionately.

The District Coordinator initiates block watches, provides training for Block Captains and at block meetings, oversees volunteer programs in their district, ensures that information received from the Administrator is distributed to the Block Captains, updates Block Captains on crime hot spots in their districts, and acts as a liaison of the Administrator to his or her District.

The District Coordinator works very closely with the Crime Prevention Administrator and the Block Captains in their District. They meet on a regular basis to exchange information such as area hot spots, new programs, special needs of their assigned District, special meetings or events, and to brainstorm about for improving or overcoming any challenges.

Responsibilities of the District Coordinator include:

1.   Working with the general public to increase awareness of the programs available.
2.   Handling incoming calls from his or her assigned District.
3.   Starting watch programs on blocks in his or her District by recruiting volunteers to be Block Captains.
4.   Reviewing the progress of watches with Block Captains.

5.   Passing on information received from the Crime Prevention Administrator and keeping his or her Block Captain up-to-date.

6.   Contacting any city agencies that need to be informed of a particular problem occurring in their District, such as a health and human resource issue, a possible drug house, etc.

7.   Arranging for training of Block Captains on a regular basis and insuring that Block Captains are distributing information to participants on their blocks.

8.   Insuring that the annual (or semi-annual) meetings are being conducted with a representative of the law enforcement department in the different blocks of his or her assigned District

9.   Arranging training on specific topics like personal safety, target hardening, etc.

10.   Recruiting officers from his or her District to assist with specialized training.

11.   Acting as chairman of the Steering Committee, if applicable.

12.   Maintaining a comprehensive list of Community Watch Block Captains and participants including addresses and phone numbers.

13.   Arranging for signs to be purchased or issued to blocks announcing that the block has a watch program in effect and installing the signs.

14.   If a Steering Committee is in place, the District Coordinator is responsible for establishing sub-committees to design specific crime prevention projects; i.e., operation identification, an evaluation of the program, block parents, etc.

15.   If there is no Steering Committee in place, then the District Coordinator will work with the Block Captains to design specific crime prevention projects like those listed in number 14.

Community Watch Steering Committee

The Community Watch Steering Committee is designed to act as a guiding force for your Community Watch program. The Program Coordinator usually serves on the Steering Committee, and usually there are two or three Block Captains so that the Community Watch leadership always has the benefit of insights from the people on the front lines.

Membership on the Steering Committee should represent a significant cross-section of the community. There should be members from the private sector as well as the public and not-for-profit sectors. Here are some groups to consider when looking for members:

- Law enforcement representatives other than the Program Coordinator
- local business leaders
- representatives of homeowners associations
- representatives the Mayor's office, city council members, or from county commissioners
- members of civic organizations like the Rotary Club, Lions Club, and Chamber of Commerce
- school and university representatives
- representatives of the various religious communities

Responsibilities of the Steering Committee

Every Steering Committee is unique. It is distinguished by the priorities of the community it serves. However, these bodies must assume the following responsibilities:

1. To determine the concerns of the community with regard to crime.

2. To ascertain from law enforcement officials the reported crimes occurring in the area.

3. To design programs, in cooperation with law enforcement, to address the concerns of the community regards to crime with and the crime reports obtained from law enforcement.

4. To advance and maintain the existing programs to include as many residents as possible.

5. To evaluate the success of programs initiated with regard to the reduction of specific crimes and the fear of crime.

6. To address other issues that concern residents that have nothing to do with crime, like fire safety, first aid, disaster preparedness, etc.

7. To design a crime victimization survey to assess the crimes occurring in the area and to create an interest in crime prevention.

Responsibilities of the Block Captain

The Block Captain's responsibility is one area, usually a street block, with the block kept as small as possible, generally between eight and ten houses facing each other. Small blocks are easier to manage and make it more likely that the neighbors will get acquainted.

The position of Block Captain should be a shared responsibility between two people or co-captains. This is done so that if one individual cannot be present for training, is out of town, or needs assistance, the job will still be done for that block. It also helps neighbors to learn to work together as a team and become better acquainted, thereby promoting more of a sense of community.

The Block Captain's responsibilities include:

1.   Distributing information through a quarterly newsletter containing updates received from the District Coordinator.

2.   Keeping the block map up-to-date, with the current names, addresses and phone numbers of the people on the block.

3.   Keeping track of the people living in each house: their profession, work phone numbers, medical problems, etc.

4.   Coordinating all activities for the block such as block meetings, block parties, etc.

5.   Insuring that any incident that takes place is immediately reported to the police or 911 has been called and making phone calls on a phone tree to others on the block.

6.   Greeting any new neighbors that move into the neighborhood, educating them about the Community Watch program providing them with a start-up package or Citizen's Guide to Community Watch, and updating the block list.

7.   Participating in the training programs conducted for Block Captains by the District Coordinator.

8.   Relaying messages received from the crime alert system if one has been set up by local law enforcement.

9.   Serving as a liaison between the District Coordinator (or Administrator) and participants in the watch program.

10.   Assigning work like: secretarial duties: fundraising to purchase signs, electric engravers, videos, written material, etc; vacation house

checks; elderly house checks; and patrols.

11.   Informing the District Coordinator if the Block Captain resigns, and having the group meet to elect a replacement.

12.   Ensuring that the District Coordinator has the Block Captain's phone numbers at home and at work.

13.   Recommending candidates to serve in the management structure of the Community Watch Program—especially as members of the Steering Committee.

Block Group Members

Finally, it's important to remember that each individual and family that agrees to participate is making a commitment to his or her neighbors. As Block Captain, you will need to be sure that each newcomer understands this and to reinforce this idea with established members.

The responsibilities of individual participants include:

1.   Learning neighbor's names and being able to recognize them and their vehicles without hesitation.

2.   Keeping a personal block map, block profile sheet, and telephone tree in an easily accessible place and updating them with new information.

3.   Attending all watch meetings.

4.   Implementing all security measures suggested by law enforcement after the home security surveys have been completed.

5.   Properly identifying all property using the guidelines suggested in Operation Identification.

6.   Keeping an eye on neighbors' homes and reporting any suspicious activities to local law enforcement and neighbors.

7.   Writing down a description of any suspicious-looking persons or vehicles and reporting them to your local law enforcement agency.

8.   Teaching children about crime prevention and about respect for law enforcement officers.

9.   Not taking any risks to prevent a crime or trying to make an arrest. It is more important to be a good witness.

10.   Having the mail and newspapers picked up or stopped when away

for extended periods.

11.   Notifying the Block Captain and neighbors of the absence so that the home can be watched.

Meetings

Meetings

Planning Meetings

Understanding how to plan and run meetings is critical to the success of your Community Watch Program. You'll have meetings with the Steering Committee, with your management team, and with Block Groups. There will also be meetings with other community organizations and meetings where you give reports to the city council, county commission or other governing bodies.

In a grassroots organization like Community Watch, you have to communicate with people efficiently about the program's goals, plans, and results. You have to provide training information to groups of people because to do it on an individual basis would be impossible. Whether you like them or not, meetings are a necessary part of your program.

This does not mean that meetings have to be boring or inefficient, nor does it mean that you must personally organize and attend all the meetings that go on in your Community Watch Program. The purpose of this section is to help you plan and organize effective, efficient meetings that help you get results. The material presented here will also enable you to train District Coordinators, Block Captains and others to plan and organize meetings, so that you don't have to do everything yourself!

Meetings are where most of the business interaction takes place between the community and you, the Block Captain. There will be social occasions when you interact as well, but you learn, discuss and make decisions as a group when meeting in fire halls, community centers, and living rooms. Because Community Watch Programs tend to hold similar types of meetings, we are going to discuss each type in some detail. These include meetings of District Coordinators and Block Captains, of the Steering Committee, of District Coordinators and Block Groups, and of Block Groups. For each situation, we provide you with generic agendas along with brief explanations of each. This will help guide you through your first few meetings.

Meetings between the District Coordinator and Block Captains

COMMENTARY: Meetings between the District Coordinator and Block Captains are designed to share information and help improve your Community Watch Program. They also function to provide training for the Block Captains and any citizens who desire further education on crime prevention practices. Such meetings provide an opportunity to conduct training on any number of different subjects to a large group of people, rather than at a block level. If you have the resources to do block training on a regular basis, then by all means do so; if not, then this is an excellent alternative.

Use these meetings to obtain feedback about concerns or challenges the Block Captains may be having, and address those issues to find a solution. These discussions will give you an opportunity to hear about the concerns of the community. Such meetings provide a good time to distribute any written material that is supposed to be passed along to the Block Captains and residents.

At a minimum, meetings between the Coordinator and Block Captains should take place once every three months. If possible, hold meetings once a month. You can always keep them short. This is essential to ensure that information and issues are addressed on a timely basis.

Use the following format for meetings between the District Coordinator and Block Captains:

BLOCK CAPTAINS MEETING AGENDA
ANYTOWN COMMUNITY WATCH
Date _____

Chaired by: District Coordinator, Program Coordinator or Assistant Program Coordinator

    1. Call the meeting to order.
    2. Discuss any new developments that need to be brought to the attention of

the Block Captains and distribute any written information.

    3. Ask Block Captains if there are any challenges they need to address, and work toward a solution with them.

    4. Conduct the training session.

    5. Adjourn the meeting.

Agenda for Exploratory Meetings

SHOULD PIPER ROAD NEIGHBORS FORM A BLOCK GROUP?
ANYTOWN COMMUNITY WATCH
Date _____

Chaired by: Acting Block Captain

1) Welcome and introductions
2) Explanation of Community Watch: What it is and why you are interested
3) Discussion: Should Lawnsdale Road Neighbors start a Block Group?
4) If yes, plan a start-up meeting: set date, time and location and agree on tentative agenda; elect co-captains create crime Prevention training presentation
5) Distribute Crime Surveys and Family Data Sheets
6) Adjourn

Block Group Meetings

    These meetings are intended to educate a Block Watch group about crime prevention and to provide training appropriate to the group's needs and interests. They also provide the forum primarily for transacting business on behalf of the group.

The initial meeting should gauge neighbor interest. It can be very short—10 to 15 minutes should be sufficient. Under no circumstances should you go longer than 30 minutes. Assuming there is significant interest, the group should schedule a start-up meeting. Hand out Family Data Sheets and Crime Surveys and ask everyone to complete these and bring them to the next meeting. If you prefer, you can also try to collect this data before the meeting so that you can start identifying key areas of neighborhood concern.

At the start-up meeting, you will choose Block Co-Captains, discuss preliminary goals and conduct an initial crime prevention training with members of your local law enforcement agency if possible. (See Start-Up Meeting Agenda below.) The training session will feature a presentation on crime prevention by the local law enforcement representative. If no representative is available, we have provided a presentation outline on the next page.

Your Block Group should meet regularly—once or twice per month. Also, you should plan on a minimum of one meeting a year between the Block Group and the District Coordinator. You should have a law enforcement representative present at your meetings at least twice a year. Take advantage of any opportunity to meet with the group to conduct training. If members request training sessions on a monthly basis and are attending regularly, find a way to ensure these meetings take place. This will keep enthusiasm high and benefit the program in the long run.

START-UP MEETING: Before your initial block meeting, distribute the Crime Survey and Family Data Sheets to the neighborhood and ask people to complete them and bring them to the meeting. When you begin the meeting, be sure to have folks sign in and ask them to briefly introduce themselves. When you come to the agenda item dealing with the Crime Survey, be prepared with extra copies for people who didn't get them or forgot to bring them. You can take this opportunity to give them a couple minutes to finish their surveys. You may need to ask whether the surveys prompted anyone to think of special training needs or concerns. Also inquire if they have arranged for a home security survey by your local law enforcement agency. This is of special concern if your department requires a certain percentage of homes to complete the survey and implement recommendations prior to receiving their Community Watch sign. If your group wishes to have training on other subjects, begin making arrangements with speakers and set dates and times for the meetings. Within one week of the first meeting, the Block Captain should have completed, copied, and distributed the block map, telephone tree, and block profile sheet.

Following is the agenda for the Block Captain's first meeting with his or her Block Group. That is followed by a suggested outline for the Crime Prevention Presentation—to be given by a law enforcement representative, if possible.

PINE STREET BLOCK GROUP
START-UP MEETING AGENDA
ANYTOWN COMMUNITY WATCH
Date _____

NOTE: Ordinarily, crime surveys and family data sheets are distributed prior to this meeting, and residents are asked to bring them.

Meeting chaired by: Block Captain

1) Circulate meeting sign-in sheet
2) Call to order, welcome and introductions
3) Overview of Block Group and Block Captain responsibilities
4) Election/appointment of Block Co-Captains
5) Brief discussion of Crime Survey and Family Data Sheet
   a) Training needs
   b) Neighborhood concerns
   c) Collect surveys and data sheets
6) Introduction of _____ (law enforcement representative)
7) Crime Prevention Presentation by _____ (law enforcement representative)
8) Announcements
   a) Inform everyone that you will complete the block map, the telephone tree and the block profile sheet, and that you will distribute them within the week.
   b) Other announcements
9) Thank everyone for attending

Crime Prevention Presentation Outline

COMMENTARY: The next section includes an outline on crime prevention that you and your local law enforcement representative should go over together prior to the Block Group training session. The purpose of this presentation is to provide neighbors with an overview of crime prevention, home security surveys, reporting suspicious activities, etc. This training session is a meeting in itself—you should not plan on doing a lot of other business at this event. Allow as much time as possible for the Block Group to learn about crime prevention and to get their questions answered. Since this meeting is extremely important to the effective launch of new Block Groups, we have developed a comprehensive outline that starts on the next page. You and your law enforcement representative should decide what modifications are required for your particular neighborhood.

AGENDA FOR LAW ENFORCEMENT REPRESENTATIVE MEETING WITH BLOCK GROUP

1.   Introduction

Introduce yourself and thank everyone for attending and for their interest in crime prevention. Thank the Chief of Police or Sheriff. (This should be done at the beginning of each program whether they are present or not.)

Give a little history of Community Watch in your community—how long it has been active and any success stories where a Watch program assisted local law enforcement.

Discuss the fact that crime prevention is the responsibility of all citizens in the community. Explain that local law enforcement people cannot be everywhere at once. They depend on the community to act as their eyes and ears, to observe and report any suspicious activities in their neighborhood.

2.   Address local concerns.

Discuss the Crime Survey results (provided by the Block Captain). Identify the greatest concern reported by survey respondents. Take some time to address this concern and discuss how an active Community Watch Program can help. Invite questions from the Block Group.

3.   Discuss the principles of crime prevention.

Crime prevention is a joint effort between law enforcement and the community to reduce crime in several ways. One way is by teaching citizens techniques to reduce the risk of being victimized at home and in public. Another way is by training citizens on the importance of recognizing suspicious activities and how to report them. Neighbors need to get to know each other and their routines so that any out-of-place activity can be reported and investigated. Another way is by teaching participants how to make their homes more secure and properly identify their property for easier recovery if stolen.

Instead of the traditional situation where law enforcement reacts after the fact, crime prevention is a more proactive approach to law enforcement. Training citizens in methods to deter crime before it occurs removes one of the key elements of crime—the opportunity for it to take place.

Crime can be deterred physically by installing lights, locks and other hardware, and by altering the landscape. There are psychological deterrents as well, like changing the way one, walks and talks, or the way in which a neighborhood appears to be cared for. Changing one's habits and awareness can help deter crime.

4.   Describe Community Watch.

Community Watch works because residents are more familiar with their neighborhoods than local law enforcement can be. The people know who lives there, what their daily routines are, and whether an activity is suspicious.

Community Watch normally consists of a city block including houses on both sides of the street or small geographical areas. Community Watch is designed this way so that participants share common visual areas in which to observe pedestrian and vehicle traffic.

Participants need to observe and report. They are never expected to take personal risks or endanger themselves in an effort to prevent a crime.

Community Watch works in our community because of four factors:

    a. The priorities of our local Community Watch Program

    b. The management structure of the program

    c. How Block Groups are initiated

    d. The requirements for receiving or maintaining a sign.

5.   Discuss suspicious activity. If you have handouts, distribute them now. Explain how to observe and report suspicious activities.

     Suspicious activity is an event taking place that is out of the ordinary or should not be occurring. Knowing your neighbors, their habits, and the composition of their households will make it easier to recognize and report any suspicious activities occurring in your neighborhood.

     When reporting suspicious activity, utilize the 911 emergency system (where available) or dial your local law enforcement agency direct. Keep the phone number of your local law enforcement agency near your phone in either case. When using the 911 emergency system, remember that there are three different types of emergencies--Police, Fire, and Medical. You may be reporting any one of these as a result of your Community Watch program.

6.   Explain how to use the following tools. (See page 40 for an explanation of each.)

          Block Map
          Block Profile Sheet
          Suspicious Activity/Crime Report
          Telephone Tree Sheet

7.   Home Security Surveys

     Home security is taking preventive measures for reducing the risk of becoming a crime victim in your home. Most burglars are not skilled professionals. Most burglaries are committed by youths 18 and under, both male and female. Burglars are looking for "easy targets," such as: unoccupied homes, open or unlocked doors and windows, homes that hide them from neighbors and passersby, and homes without adequate locks or lighting. Thieves are looking for items easily sold for cash that have no identifying numbers or marks.

     Weekday daylight hours are the most popular time for residential burglaries. Most burglaries occur in homes where a door or window wasn't locked.

     By taking some simple, precautionary steps, you can reduce the chances of becoming a crime victim in your home. Lock doors and windows. The best locks are no good if they're not used. Leave the lights on at night over doorways and garages. Replace inadequate locks and light.

Make your home appear occupied at all times. Keep shrubbery trimmed so that it doesn't conceal burglars. Never hide keys under the doormat or in the mailbox. Leave the keys with a trusted friend. Do not leave notes on the door explaining your absence. Ensure cash on hand is kept to a minimum. Place seldom used valuables in a safe deposit box. Frequently worn jewelry should not be kept in your bedroom.

Keep valuables away from windows where they can be seen. Television sets, VCRS, computers and DVDs invite burglars. Place a permanent identification number on any valuables kept at your home. Discuss your state's method of identifying personal property.

Your checkbook, credit cards and similar documents should be in a locked drawer. Likewise, you should secure your financial records, social security card, and any other documents that might be attractive to identity thieves.

Don't carry identification tags on your keys. If you lose them a burglar may be able to identify where you live.

Hand out the Home Security Survey form (see appendix). Discuss what will take place during the survey, i.e., making suggestions about how to secure their homes more effectively by installing better lighting, locks, doors, landscaping, etc. Let them know that many of the changes that may be recommended are relatively inexpensive. It is important to keep in mind that many of the people in the Block Group may not be able to afford the best material on the market. Instead of stating this and looking bad, they may not schedule an appointment. Or, after the survey, they may not implement the recommendations.

Discuss scheduling a security survey. Included on the Home Security Survey Sheet is a space for scheduling a time and date for a survey. If you can set appointments now while the interest level and enthusiasm are high.

If appropriate, discuss the option of using video or digital photographs to document household contents for crime prevention purposes. Having photos or tape is also great for insurance or estate purposes.

Each state views such surveys differently. Each has different laws governing public records laws. Be sure to go into the meeting with the correct information for your state.

8.   Operation Identification. The Household Inventory form is a useful handout to accompany this program (see appendix).

Burglars sell what they steal for cash, often to support a drug habit. This makes it difficult for law enforcement to trace stolen items. The stolen items look like hundreds of others. Therefore, unless there is a way to prove that an item belongs to you, law enforcement can't return it to you.

By marking your property and keeping an inventory, you will be able to prove that the stolen items are yours and law enforcement will be able to return those items to you.

Use an electric engraving pen or an inexpensive, diamond-tipped marking pen to identify property. Use only a diamond-marking pen on computers and peripherals. Photograph jewelry and other valuables. (If your law enforcement department loans engraving pens, inform the Block Group of this.)

Mark your possessions in a place that's difficult to cover or remove. Use your last name as the identifier, or consult with your local law enforcement agency for alternatives. In the past it was common to use a driver's license number to identify property, but because of concerns over identity theft, this is less desirable than it once was.

If an item is a piece of power equipment, like a riding mower, mark it on both the engine and the chassis. Often these items are taken apart and put together with other similar types of equipment.

Make an Inventory List of all your valuables and marked property. If the items are too small or unmarkable, take photographs or videotape them. Keep the Inventory List and the photographs or videotape along with other important papers in a bank safe deposit box.

Remember that these suggestions only work if they are implemented. The best lock keeps unwanted intruders out only if it's locked. There are no guarantees that your home won't be burglarized, even if you follow all of these suggestions. However, the chances of being a crime victim are significantly reduced if these crime prevention recommendations are followed. If you haven't already, take these suggestions and begin doing your part to fight crime in your community.

9. Future meeting topics

The following list provides you with a variety of topics that can be addressed at future meetings:

- Personal Safety
- Gangs
- Fraud and Con Games
- Identity Theft

- Child Safety
- Drug Abuse Prevention
- Domestic Violence
- Sexual Abuse
- Gun Safety
- CPR and First Aid
- Larceny Prevention
- Selecting and Installing Locking Devices
- Self Defense
- Safety Tips for Senior Citizens
- Annoying Telephone Calls
- Safety Tips for Baby Sitters
- Recognizing Substance Abuse
- Vandalism Prevention
- Fire Prevention

Potential sources for training on the above topics include local law enforcement agencies; state and federal agencies dealing with law enforcement, postal inspection, mental health, aging, etc.; as well as nonprofit and commercial organizations dealing with home security and insurance.

Generic Agenda for Subsequent Block Meetings

Subsequent Block Group meetings will be conducted by the Block Captain and will tend to conform to an agenda similar to the one shown below.

STEERING COMMITTEE AGENDA
ANYTOWN COMMUNITY WATCH
Date _____

Meeting chaired by Block Captain

1. Call to order; welcome and introductions
2. Review agenda and modify as needed
3. Financial report

4. Old business
5. New business
6. Adjourn

Block Group Training Meetings

These are special Block Group meetings that focus on topics group members identify as priorities. Because of the variety of subjects that can be addressed, we have provided a basic agenda that you can modify as needed. The District Coordinator will need to prepare the specific topic for presentation.

PINE STREET BLOCK GROUP TRAINING MEETING
ANYTOWN COMMUNITY WATCH
Date _____

Chaired by: District Coordinator, Program Coordinator, or Block Captain.

1. Introduce presenter and topic
2. Discuss topic
3. Conduct question and answer period
4. Thank group for attending

Community Presentations

From time to time, you will receive invitations to make presentations about the Community Watch Program. Ordinarily, such presentations to community or civic organizations are designed to promote crime prevention and/or obtain support from the group. Take advantage of these opportunities.

It has been said that "action creates enthusiasm." The more people hear you talking about Community Watch, the more people will come forward with enthusiasm. Let local groups know that you are available to speak on crime prevention. It's important that you prepare your presentation in advance. The main points that need to be conveyed are the history of crime prevention efforts in the community, what effect it has had or can have on reducing crime, and what the group can do to advance these efforts. It's also important that you customize this presentation to your community's need and the program you have developed. It would be impossible for this book to produce the perfect presentation for each situation you will encounter, so use the main points outlined below as a guideline.

The following is a possible presentation. For your convenience, we have furnished a complete outline. Some parts duplicate material presented earlier in this section.

COMMUNITY WATCH AND CRIME PREVENTION IN ANYTOWN

(Presentation Outline)

I. Introduce yourself and thank the group members for allowing you to speak about crime prevention.

II. Give a short history of Community Watch in your community—how long it has been active, any success stories where a watch program assisted local law enforcement with apprehending a suspect, etc.

III. Discuss the fact that crime prevention is the responsibility of every citizen in the community. Explain that local law enforcement officers cannot be everywhere at once and that they depend on the community to act as their eyes and ears, to observe and report any suspicious activities in the neighborhood.

IV. Discuss the principles of crime prevention.

A. Crime prevention is a partnership between law enforcement, other government agencies, and the community. It is everyone's business.

B. Crime prevention works at solving social problems in addition to addressing crime problems.

C. Crime prevention saves money for taxpayers.

D. Crime prevention should be a primary concern of law enforcement.

E. Crime prevention includes educating the community about how to remove the opportunity for a crime to be committed.

F. Crime prevention addresses the specific concerns of a community.

G. Crime prevention requires re-evaluation of programs in order to improve them.

V. Describe Community Watch.

A. Community Watch works because residents are more familiar with their neighborhoods than local law enforcement officers are. Residents know who lives there, what their daily routines are, and whether an activity is truly suspicious.

B. Community Watch normally consists of a city block including houses on both sides of the street or other small geographical areas. It is designed this way so that participants share common visual areas to observe pedestrian and vehicle traffic.

C. Participants are expected to observe and report—not to take personal risks or endanger themselves in any way to prevent a crime.

D. How Community Watch works in your community. Discuss any requirements for receiving a sign from the city or for retaining a sign already in place.

E. Tal about what the organization as a whole can do to help. If you are looking for monetary donations, let them know now. Ask if some of the members of the organization would like to start block watches in their neighborhoods.

F. Thank them for any support they can give and for allowing you to speak to them about crime prevention.

Keeping Meetings Focused

By having a clear purpose in mind and having a well-organized agenda, you will find that meetings run according to plan and produce positive outcomes. Occasionally things happen that are out of your control and you need to be ready when that happens. For example, it's a virtual certainty that people will want to discuss topics in more detail, and you will have to make a decision about how rigidly to stick to your original agenda and schedule.

We recommend you maintain a certain degree of flexibility when this happens. The way to do this is to not overcrowd your agenda. Plan on the possibility of people having questions or wanting to discuss things in more detail. By allowing for that, you can comfortably let the discussion go on for a couple minutes here and there and then gently but firmly steer it back to the next item on the agenda.

Meetings have been known to get out of control because someone comes in with a complaint or wants to monopolize the discussion. To prevent this from happening, you will need a strategy. We suggest you begin your meeting by telling the audience what you plan to cover. Distribute copies of the agenda, or write it on an easel for everyone to see. Get a sense of what people are most concerned about, or if there's anything else they have questions about. Some people will be content with whatever you have planned. Others will have an interest in a particular item on the agenda and you may want to adjust the time allocated to that topic. Still others may have an interest or concern completely apart from what's on the agenda.

By letting people see in advance what the plan is, you achieve two things: 1) You give them some say in the meeting so that it more directly deals with the things they are interested in; and 2) you determine the most appropriate way to handle potential distractions. As for how to handle the unanticipated questions and topics that come up, here are some suggestions:

- If it's a very simple question asking for simple information, deal with it now and get on with the rest of the meeting.
- If it's relevant to the meeting, but you're not there yet, tell them there will be an opportunity to discuss it later when you get to that topic on the agenda.
- If it's not relevant to the meeting, you can add it as a topic to bring up under New Business, discuss it after the meeting, or agree to address it at the next meeting.

Your role as the meeting facilitator is to address the business that has been planned while being attentive to the needs and concerns of the attendees. That requires a balance between sticking to your planned agenda and finding ways to accommodate the inevitable distractions and questions. By allowing a reasonable amount of time in your agenda to accommodate these situations, you give yourself freedom to be flexible and everybody's needs are met. The participants see that you operate with a sense of fairness and focus on results. They will appreciate both your flexibility and your focus in sticking to the agenda.

Communication

Communication

The success of a Community Watch program rests in the leader's ability to effectively communicate the ideas and principles of Community Watch to others and to motivate them to take action.

Communication is the transfer of ideas between individuals. The whole purpose of Community Watch is to transfer ideas about crime prevention and other civic issues to people in the community. The community needs to know about the concepts of crime prevention in order for Community Watch to be successful.

Educating people about Community Watch and crime prevention is only the first step. The next step is to motivate those people to take action and implement the ideas conveyed. If residents do not take action on the suggestions you have communicated, then no Community Watch Program will exist.

People communicate in many ways—through writing, speaking, drawing and body gestures. In each method they are trying to convey an idea. Strive to build these effective communication skills throughout your career as Program Coordinator. Following are a few simple steps to improve your communication skills.

1. Be sure that your message is clear and easily understood. The best way to accomplish this is to communicate your message in the manner best suited to the individuals receiving it. People are more receptive to what is familiar to them. People have a tendency to reject or ignore what is new or different.

You are already adding a relatively new dimension to your audience's thinking when talking about crime prevention, so stay on their level of communication by conveying your message in a language that recipients will understand. Be sure not to talk down to people, which can shut off the receptivity of the listener. In this case communication will not take place. If the message is not understood, then your time and energy have been wasted.

2. Be sure to talk or write in understandable terms. Don't use jargon or law enforcement lingo without giving a clear and precise definition to the audience. Explaining each term people may not understand. The use of unfamiliar terms causes confusion and the recipient of your message may tune you out altogether.

3. Listen. One of the most important and often overlooked aspects of good communication is listening to those with whom you are communicating. Listen to what others are telling you through their speech, writing, and body language. Listening provides a means to gauge how well you are communicating your point so that you can clarify yourself if necessary.

Effective listening requires that you focus attention on the speaker. One way to do this is to watch the speaker while he or she is speaking. Also make sure you are in a position to adequately hear what is being said. It is important to comprehend what the speaker has communicated to you. In communicating, the message sent is not as important as the message received. If the message is interpreted out of the context in which it was sent, then effective communication has not taken place.

One way to be sure that you understand what the speaker is saying, is to repeat back what you perceive as the message. If the message is wrong, then a correction can be made, and you will be able to respond appropriately. Another way to make your listening more effective is to pay attention to the behavior of others. In police work, observing the behavior of others is critical. It gives you an idea of exactly what is taking place around you. Knowing the concerns of the individual or group of people you are addressing will provide you with information to communicate more effectively.

It's obvious that if you are addressing a group of people and half of them are asleep, they are not receiving your message. Pay attention to the messages they are sending—messages like a look of confusion or body language like crossed arms or eyes wandering that indicate people are not paying attention. If you find this is happening, you may want to ask if there are any questions, or check to see if the discussion is dragging on longer than expected. Another way to regain attention is to tell a joke or an interesting story. Laughter makes people more receptive to the message you are communicating and people enjoy hearing a story. The best teachers use stories to get their points across.

4. Avoid surprises. If there's criminal activity occuring, you need to see to it that everyone in your program knows about it before they hear it on the radio or read about it in the newspaper. Tell your District Coordinators and Block Captains and make sure that they relay the message to everyone else. Make it your mission to put each Community Watch participant is in a "first-to-know" position

If there are program changes, make sure people up the chain of responsibility are informed. Chiefs of Police and Sheriffs, especially, must not be blind-sided. Keep them informed. If one of your Community Watch volunteers offers information about a crime or suspicious activity, make sure it gets to the proper authorities. "I have solved major cases based on such information," a crime prevention officer tells us, "and I've acquired information for other officers and detectives so that they could solve their cases. The information always came from a proven source: the neighborhood crime watcher."

At the same time, ask everyone working with you to reciprocate on this principle. As the Community Watch Coordinator, you obviously need to know about significant problems or developments. We'll say it here and we'll say it again later: Communication is a two-way process!

5. Maintain a professional appearance. One of the most important goals when conducting a presentation is to maintain a professional appearance. Most law enforcement agencies have an established policy regarding appearance.

First impressions are important. Many of the people you deal with may not be familiar with law enforcement officers and representatives. How you look, talk, and listen will influence the impression you make on your audience. How you look will affect how people listen and respond to what you are saying. People judge by appearance. If someone is distracted by the fact that your clothes are wrinkled, he or she is not paying attention to the message you are trying to convey and your purpose for being there is defeated. Some individuals may also discredit your authority as an expert based on your appearance. Keep appearance in mind when conducting presentations in the community. Making a good impression will build rapport and trust.

Being able to effectively utilize all of the communication tools available to you will ensure a successful watch program. For more effective communication, practice the methods discussed below. They too, are tools for making your Community Watch Program more successful.

Different Forms of Communication

Your program will communicate with the public in a number of different ways. Meetings with block groups and community organizations are two of the most common methods. However, there are also the media, newsletters, the Internet, your District Coordinators and Block Captains, and the Steering Committee to get your message across. The following portions of this section discuss in detail some of the different tools for communicating your message to the community.

Meetings are where most of the communication between law enforcement and the community will take place. This is why so many departments have community relations officers or community services divisions. Meetings are designed specifically for communicating. You are informing and teaching residents about crime prevention as it relates to them, and they are informing you about their concerns and needs. Working together through effective communication is the best way to solve challenges and address concerns. And meetings, whether with a Block Group, a community organization, or the Steering Committee, are an ideal place to solve problems and address challenges.

The nature of each meeting is different because topics and attendees vary. This variety will present different challenges at each meeting, but being knowledgeable about the material you are presenting allow you to adjust to each situation as it arises. (Meeting agendas for various groups are contained in the Meetings chapter.)

Presentations

Knowing the material you are going to cover and being prepared ahead of time are two essential ingredients to a successful presentation. Have your presentation thoroughly planned and practice what you are going to discuss. This will ensure you are comfortable with the material, put you more at ease, and produce a more successful presentation.

The media

Using mass media to communicate with the community as a whole is one of the most productive methods available to you. Communicating by mass media reaches the most people with the least amount of individual effort. This saves time and money.

TV and radio broadcasters are generally willing to work with you to promote your program. Many of your announcements will be run at little or no cost if you understand the needs of media professionals and how to work with them. Consider using television to help you in your efforts. With the rise of community access, government and cable access programming, you can reach many people through this popular form of communication. Be sure to promote your television programs in your newsletter and other communications.

Communication within the management structure

Meetings between the Program Coordinator, District Coordinators, and Block Captains are a vital link in communication between the Program Coordinator and the community as a whole. It is imperative to know what is happening in your community at all times so that information can be processed quickly, challenges overcome promptly, and the public alerted to important occurrences immediately. Besides allowing you to stay informed and updated on what is happening throughout the city, you will be able to ensure that the District Coordinators and Block Captains are doing their jobs as outlined in their job descriptions. This will also allow you to handle any challenges that arise in a specific district like a lack of cooperation between a city agency and the District Coordinator.

Maintaining an open line of communication between the District Coordinator and Block Captains will provide feedback about the concerns of the community, so that they can be addressed in a timely and effective manner.

We can't overemphasize that good communication is the key to an effective Community Watch Program. Meet with your District Coordinators/Block Captains on a regular basis to ensure everyone gets vital information. (Agendas for meetings with District Coordinators and Block Captains are included in the Meetings chapter.)

Electronic communications

A computerized calling machine is designed to call a preprogrammed telephone number, and deliver a specific message. If the person receiving the call wishes to respond, he can do so by leaving a reply message for the person or organization that initiated the call. A tool of this sort would be invaluable because of the number of block watches that could be contacted concerning some important issue. The amount of time saved alerting a specific neighborhood, district, or even an entire town would be quite substantial.

The use of a calling machine could apply to more than the Community Watch Program. If an emergency arose and police officers needed to be called in, the machine would be able to contact them. Potential applications of this machine include:

- rapidly disseminating important information to the community
- quickly and efficiently distributing a suspect's description to a specific neighborhood
- alerting residents about an emergency situation in their area
- broadcasting public awareness information
- notifying officers that an emergency situation exists and instructing them to report to the department as soon as possible
- notifying group members about a meeting
- gathering evidence

It's easy to see that modern technology can be used to your advantage. Utilize the tools you have. Remember that communication is the key to a successful Community Watch Program. If there is a way to communicate faster and more efficiently, by all means use it.

Newsletters and flyers

An effective form of communicating with participants at all levels of Community Watch is through the use of newsletters. Newsletters are employed by many law enforcement departments with successful watch programs. Newsletters inform participants about instances of crime watch groups that have helped law enforcement stop crime; awards given to volunteers or citizens; profiles of volunteers or law enforcement officers, suspects wanted by law enforcement; and any special events that may be taking place in the near future.

Newsletters keep participants up-to-date on Community Watch and all that is happening within their district or town. Distributing the newsletter provides a reason for District Coordinators to contact Block Captains, and Block Captains to call on participants. This helps assure that communication occurs at all levels of your Community Watch Program.

Sometimes individuals become involved in Community Watch and attend an initial meeting but are never contacted again. Providing a newsletter to distribute will give the Coordinator and Block Captains a reason to contact participants. This keeps the participants up-to-date on the Watch Program, even if the group isn't meeting on a regular basis.

What the newsletter should contain

The newsletter does not need to be an elaborate production to be effective. It is a tool for communication and as long as it is doing this effectively, that is what matters. The purpose of the newsletter is to inform participants about the events relating to Community Watch occurring in their area.

Here are a few recommended subjects to include in your newsletter: crime hot spots, volunteer profiles, awards presented to volunteers or citizens, a story on crime prevention, and a letter from the Program Coordinator. Because of recent international events, you may also consider offering a regular update on the war on terrorism and how localities are responding. The following are some specific ideas for stories you might want to include in your newsletter:

A feature story about prevention, security, safety, etc. This sets the theme of the newsletter by discussing a topic that relates to crime prevention such as home security or personal safety.

A feature story about a volunteer. Volunteers are one of the most crucial elements in a successful Community Watch Program. As discussed in the volunteer section of this manual, volunteers need to be recognized for their efforts and contributions frequently. A story profiling one of the volunteers involved with your program will encourage the volunteer being profiled, inspire other volunteers participating in the program, and encourage others in the community to become involved with Community Watch as a participant or volunteer.

Award presentations. Recognition of volunteers cannot be stressed enough. Any time an award or some form of recognition is given to a resident of the community, be sure to include this item in the newsletter. It also encourages the volunteer being profiled, inspires other volunteers in the program, and encourages participation from others in the community to become involved with Community Watch. Recognition of this type is vital to ensure the longevity of your Community Watch Program and the continued motivation of participants and volunteers. It is always encouraging to know that your efforts have been appreciated by others.

Citizen involvement in preventing or thwarting crime. A detailed account of the circumstances surrounding the incident, along with a picture of the individual who performed the noteworthy deed and a law enforcement representative, is an effective way to present this type of story. This is also a way to reward the individual for his or her effort to do something good for the community. With all of the negative press today, you have a chance to show the positive side of people and encourage others to do something to make a difference.

List of suspects wanted by law enforcement. This could be composite drawings or pictures of the suspects with pertinent data to accompany them. If the suspect is apprehended because of this list, write about it in the newsletter. This helps the community understand that these programs can make a difference.

Phone numbers for reporting information about crimes or crime suspects, child abuse hotlines, rape hotline, health and human resources, drug enforcement agency, and the department's phone numbers are some that should be included. Be consistent with your listings so that residents know where to look to find these numbers. Listing these applicable phone numbers reinforces them in readers' minds every time they read the newsletter.

Description of a crime prevention program and how it works. A small feature discussing a program like child safety or a safe home program is another effective method for teaching participants about crime prevention, safety, and what other programs that are available to the community.

A story about an unsolved crime. A detailed story about a major, unsolved crime in the area can assist you to learn more about the case and help to solve it. This also involves the citizens and promotes open communication between law enforcement and the community.

Other community programs your readers should know about. Programs such as fire or boat safety, workshops on first aid and CPR, and presentations about Citizens Corp and Community Emergency Response Teams (CERT) can be listed in the newsletter with dates, times, and locations. Discuss how Community Watch addresses these other programs and show the relationship between Community Watch and other issues. Limiting your newsletter to crime prevention will not utilize this communication tool to its fullest potential.

Remember that Community Watch is designed to benefit the community as a whole. Addressing issues other than crime prevention takes in the entire scope of the community's needs. Some newsletters will even address social issues--

such as promoting family unity--by listing activities that families can do together. It's important for the community to understand that crime can be the result of a multitude of problems and how participating in Community Watch will address those concerns.

A simple example of how Community Watch addresses other concerns A fire starts outside a home late at night on a block active in Community Watch. A neighbor across the street notices the fire before the homeowner does, and because the neighbor has learned how to report an emergency, and because the neighbor has a completed block map with the exact address of the neighbor, the fire is extinguished promptly before serious damage is done. Because the neighbor had the homeowner's phone number, the homeowner was called and warned to get out of the house. The neighbors living next door were also warned about the fire and were able to move their families to safety.

This example may seem simple, but many of the individuals who read the newsletter will see a practical benefit for Community Watch. This will tend to reinforce their commitment to your program.

Announcement of grants and contributions. If your department is asking the community for donations for a McGruff (tm) costume, and a local service organization donates $300 towards the purchase, note that in the newsletter. This will encourage other groups to do the same and give the group that donated the money the positive recognition it deserves.

A section devoted to teenagers and younger children. The teenage section could be written by a teenage volunteer. The teenage section can discuss ways for teenagers to participate in crime prevention and the programs that are available to them. Meanwhile, the children's section could have games to play and drawings to color. This is an effective method for communicating the message of crime prevention to children.

Having these sections will encourage young people to read the newsletter and provide them with important information about personal safety and crime prevention. It will also encourage their participation in your program. By the way, keep in mind that the Boy Scouts offer a merit badge for crime prevention. This will provide a natural audience for your newsletter--and a good place to seek out volunteers!

A listing of crime hot spots. This is one of the most important sections in the entire newsletter. Making the community aware of crime sprees will allow it to be on the lookout for specific, suspicious activity in the area and increase the chance of reporting the crime and apprehending the criminal. When community members are knowledgeable about crime activity, they are better prepared to prevent it and thereby the fear of crime is reduced.

A profile of an officer. This is an excellent public relations tool. Most people look up to police officers. Profiling an officer allows the community to become better acquainted with the department as a whole, produces a sense of familiarity, and will build trust between the department and the community. Include a short background of the officer, his/her years with the department, his or her specialty, and a short description of duties. Recount an interesting call that he or she has responded to. Be sure to include a picture if possible.

Crime Stoppers reports. If your community has Crime Stoppers, the newsletter should include highlights from this program. Reports and statistics about cases solved help to demonstrate the difference an involved citizenry can make. Some Crime Stopper programs produce crime re-enactments for television starring Crime Stopper or Community Watch members. This would be a good story to share in your newsletter.

Printing your newsletter

Remember that your newsletter does not need to be an elaborate production. Some law enforcement departments have their newsletter printed on newsprint by a commercial printer. Others print theirs off their computer and copy it. It's a good idea to have a volunteer assist you in putting the newsletter together. Newsletters do require time for both writing and layout.

You may choose to sell advertising in the paper to offset the cost of printing. When you're discussing advertising with local businesses, keep in mind that if they advertise in your newsletter, they will portray themselves as supporters of crime prevention and create goodwill for themselves in the community. You may even be able to have the printing donated by the print shop in return for a mention in the newsletter.

Labels with the addresses of participants and Block Captains can be generated for the mailing. However, this can be costly depending on the number of individuals on the mailing list.

Remember that the distribution process can provide an opportunity for the District Coordinators, Block Captains, and participants to touch base.

Following are a few ideas on different methods for putting together a newsletter.

Newspaper style (Tabloid). This is generally 12" x 15", folds, and is printed on newsprint. If this is the type of newsletter you would like, discuss it with a local printer who can provide assistance with the layout. (Feel free to use the Community Watch mastheads at the end of this section.). A tabloid is the most expensive form of newsletter and because of that, departments usually sell advertising in the paper to offset the cost.

8 1/2" x 11" Folded Newsletter (11"x17" paper size). An 8 1/2" x 11" folded newsletter is actually printed on 11" x 17" paper and folded in half. This is just a step down from the newspaper type and can be expanded to include a number of articles and stories. This type of newsletter is also easy to produce using an office computer, setting up and printing each 8 1/2" x 11" page, then taking all of them to the printer to set up and copy. The printer can even fold the final copies for you so that all you have to do is distribute them. Many of the newer photocopiers can also be used to produce this format.

8 1/2" x 11" Sheet. An 8 1/2" x 11" sheet can either be printed on one or both sides of the sheet. This is a very simple newsletter that again can be produced on your office computer, and is easy to produce, low in cost, and easily distributed.

5 1/2" x 8 1/2" Sheet Folded (8 1/2"x11" paper size). The 5 1/2" x 8 1/2" sheet folded in half is similar in design to the 8 1/2" x 11" folded sheet. This newsletter can be produced on your office computer, provided that you have a program that allows you to do so. If there isn't a lot of material in your newsletter, you may reduce a full 8 1/2" x 11" sheet with a copying machine so that the information will fit on half of a regular (8 1/2" x 11") sheet of paper. Another page is reduced to fit on the other half of the paper and the paper is folded in half. There are generally three to four sheets inside of a cover sheet that has a logo or masthead. (See samples at end of this section.)

The Internet

For some people, communicating in person or at a meeting is the best way to give them information about the program. For others, a periodic newsletter is the answer. Still others can be reached by phone.

Today, however, more than half of U.S. households have access to the Internet. Chances are that most of your Community Watch participants have household computers and use them on a regular basis. This opens the door to new communication options for your program.

Here is an excellent opportunity for you to involve community volunteers. If you put out an inquiry to your program participants, you will almost surely discover several knowledgeable people who have the interest and skill to help you implement an Internet component to Community Watch. With your volunteers, and of course with Steering Committee oversight, you can explore a number of strategies for using the Information Superhighway. The following are some of the possibilities:

1. Develop an electronic mailing list. As you collect address and contact information about program participants, don't forget to ask for e-mail addresses. Develop e-mail rosters of your District Coordinators, Block Captains, and other participants. Using this information, you can create group e-mail lists that permit you to route information quickly to program participants.

However, you need to follow some precautions when implementing such a distribution system. First, ask for permission to include participants on an electronic mailing list. Give them the choice of opting out. Second, use this distribution method sparingly. Messages sent to the group should be concerned solely with the business of your Community Watch and they should carry information that is of importance to the group as a whole. Third, take precautions to keep the e-mail addresses—as well as all information collected about your Community Watch participants—confidential. Finally, remember that the Internet is no substitute for face-to-face communication when it comes to developing good working and social relationships with the people in your community.

2. Develop a website for your Community Watch Program. With your own website, you can include information similar to what you include in your newsletter, but you can do a lot more. You can post late-breaking news in between newsletters. You can provide links to knowledgeable prevention and safety experts. You can provide access to forms and documents for your Block Captains. You can provide links to other Community Watch Programs around the world! You can provide tutorials on prevention and safety topics ranging from home security and personal safety to identity theft and Internet safety for kids.

3. Develop a bulletin board where Community Watch participants can have an ongoing dialog with each other about topics that concern them. An electronic bulletin board is like a conversation between several people who want to share ideas and exchange information. They enter the conversation electronically from the comfort of their own homes, view what's already been said, add their two cents, pose questions when they need information, and then sign off until next time.

4. Establish links between your website to other Community Watch Programs around the world. Interest in community policing is strong in many countries and by becoming more aware of what other groups are doing, you can gain some excellent ideas to use in your own program as well as make friends around the country and the world.

These are just a few ideas to start with. Get a group together and brainstorm some other possibilities. One final thing to remember is that you will still need to maintain other modes of communication in your program, first because some people might not have computers or prefer not to participate in an electronic system. Second, if you have information or announcements that are urgent or that you want to be certain reach the intended persons, telephone and face-to-face contact are always more reliable than electronic communication.

Knowing Your Neighborhood

Knowing Your Neighborhood

Why should you know your neighborhood? Because getting to know your neighbors, their families, their habits, the cars they drive, their phone numbers both at home and at work, any medical problems, and what kind of pets they have is probably one of the most important aspects of a successful Community Watch Program.

Knowing these aspects of your neighbors' lives will allow you to respond accurately and quickly to any emergency situation, and may thereby prevent a crime or save a life. The Community Watch system offers a variety of tools to help support you in your efforts.

Family Data Sheet

It's important that you share as much information as you can with your neighbors about yourself so they can recognize when something suspicious is occurring at your home.

This can be accomplished by using the Family Data Sheet. This sheet is designed to list all members of the family, their ages, telephone numbers, emergency contacts, any medical problems, family vehicles and pets, and any other information that may be helpful to emergency responders.

The Family Data Sheet will also help you in preparing the Block Map and Block Profile Sheet for distribution. (The Family Data Sheet, Block Map, Block Profile Sheet, and Telephone Tree are located at the end of this handbook.)

The Block Map

The Block Map gives you a visual perspective of your block. It's an easy reference guide to the residents on your block and can be used to explain the layout of your block when reporting an emergency situation to 911 or a law enforcement dispatcher.

The Block Captain completes the Block Map and distributes it to all participants after the start-up meeting. For each participating property, the Block Map includes: house color, address, name of resident(s) telephone number, street names and numbers, and a directional compass. You may also wish to use symbols as a visual reminder of alarms, dogs, peoples' work schedules, etc.

When distributing the Block Map to your neighbors, ask them to keep it in a place that's easily accessible to the family, yet safe from strangers.

The Block Profile Sheet

This is a more detailed record of your block's composition. It includes information such as work schedules, emergency phone numbers, types of vehicles, and health information. It also identifies special knowledge and skills of block participants that could be useful in an emergency. The Block Profile Sheet should be kept with the Block Map.

Telephone Tree

This sheet is designed so that each home in the block group will be contacted if any suspicious activity is reported. It can also be used in emergencies, or when general information needs to be communicated in a timely manner to the entire group.

The Telephone Tree provides a way to communicate quickly with every participant in the watch program. Each person on the sheet is designated to call 1 or 2 homes until all homes have been notified. When you distribute copies of the Telephone Tree, you need to be sure participants understand that it is important to keep calling the homes they have been assigned, until the contacts are successful or the emergency is over. This would make an excellent training topic for a Block meeting.

To design your Telephone Tree, list the Block Captain in the top block and fill the other blocks in with the rest of the participants of the watch program. (If you have Co-Captains, list them both in the top blocks on the sheet.) When new participants join the watch program, their names are added at the bottom of the phone tree. A good place for the Telephone Tree is on the back of the Block Map.

Here are some guidelines for using the Telephone Tree:

1.   If you're in an emergency situation, call 911 first and report what is occurring. If it is not an emergency or you have already called 911, then contact the person at the top of the list. This should be the Block Captain or one of the Co-Captains.

2.   It is the Block Captain's responsibility to ask the initial caller if he or she has contacted 911 before calling the others on the Telephone Tree.

3.   When someone on the Telephone Tree contacts you, write the message down. Read it back to the caller to verify that you got it down correctly. This ensures that you will pass along a consistent message.

4.   Start calling the household(s) directly under you. If you are unable to reach those directly below you, contact the homes next in line. Continue calling those homes that weren't contacted until they are reached.

5.   The homes at the bottom of the Tree are to call the individual at the top to indicate they have received the message. This closes the loop of communication.

6.   Note: It's a good idea to practice calling on the Telephone Tree to work out any glitches in the procedure.

Reporting Suspicious Activities

Suspicious activity is anything that is out of the ordinary or should not be occurring. Knowing your neighbors, their habits, and the composition of their households will make it easier to recognize and report any suspicious activities occurring in your neighborhood.

As Block Captain, it is your job to be sure you understand the fine points of observing and reporting suspicious activity, so that you can help the others on your block understand them as well.

How to Report Suspicious Activity

When reporting suspicious activity, use the 911 emergency system or dial your local law enforcement agency direct. Keep the phone number of your local law enforcement agency near your phone in either case. Use the Suspicious Activity/ Crime Report Sheet (located in the back of this handbook) to help you provide an accurate description of what happened.

Using the 911 Emergency System

There are three different types of emergencies: Police, Fire, and Medical. You may be reporting any one of these as part of your Community Watch program.

How to use 911 properly

1.   State clearly what kind of assistance you need: Police, Fire, or Medical.
2.   Stay on the phone and answer all questions. *Do not hang up until the dispatcher tells you to*! Follow the directions of the dispatcher. He or she is trained for emergency situations and will guide you through the entire process.
3.   Give your specific location. Use your block map to give a neighbor's address if necessary.
4.   Be sure to remain calm and to speak clearly. The 911 dispatcher may ask you for the following information: your name, address, and phone number; and what is happening. If it is a crime, he or she may ask for: a description of the suspect or suspect's vehicle; the direction he or she is heading; and the vehicle's license number.
5.   Keep the block map close by to give exact addresses and directions.
6.   Emergency calls are prioritized according to the degree that persons or property are being threatened. A crime in progress receives a quicker response than one that was committed in the past.

Why Use 911

Responding quickly and accurately is important. A large number of arrests are made as a result of information that was provided by citizens. The apprehension of one criminal, especially a burglar, may be the key to solving other crimes and reducing future crimes. Others in your community will greatly appreciate your efforts.

The time it takes to respond to a crime in progress is a determining factor in the apprehension of a criminal. A delay in reporting a crime greatly reduces law enforcement effectiveness. Commit to calling in *all* suspicious activity without delay. Better to call in a few mistakes than to have one person on your watch become the victim of a crime.

Family Disaster Planning

Disaster can strike quickly and without warning. It can force you to evacuate your neighborhood or confine you to your home. What would you do if basic services—water, gas, electricity, or telephones—were cut off? Local officials and relief workers will be on the scene after a disaster, but they cannot reach everyone right away. In fact, there have been many cases where people went without emergency services for many hours or even days following a disaster. Experts say that you and your neighbors should be fully prepared to function on your own for at least 72 hours. What follows is a plan to help you get ready to do just that.

Four Steps to Safety

Four Steps to Safety is a plan of action that you and your family can follow to prepare for an emergency. It is based on the "Family Disaster Plan" developed by the Federal Emergency Management Agency and the American Red Cross. For more information, consult these websites: www.fema.gov and www.redcross.org. At the end of this book is a reproducible Emergency Supplies List and a checklist for conducting your own Home Hazard Hunt.

1. Find out what could happen to you.

- Contact your local Red Cross chapter or emergency management office before a disaster occurs—be prepared to take notes.
- Ask what types of disasters are most likely to happen in your area. Request information on how to prepare for each one.
- Learn about your community's warning signals: what they sound like and what you should do when you hear them.
- Ask about animal care after a disaster. Animals are not allowed inside emergency shelters because of health regulations.
- Find out how to help elderly or disabled persons.
- Find out about the disaster plans at your workplace, your children's school or day care center, and other places where your family spends time.

2. Create a disaster plan.

- Meet with your family and discuss why you need to prepare for disaster. Explain the dangers of fire, severe weather, and earthquakes to children. Plan to share responsibilities and work together as a team.
- Discuss the types of disasters that are most likely to happen and explain what to do in each case.
- Pick two places to meet: right outside your home in case of a sudden emergency, like a fire; and outside your neighborhood in case you can't return home. Everyone must know the address and phone number.
- Ask an out-of-state friend to be your "family contact." After a disaster, it's often easier to call long distance. Other family members should call this person and tell him or her where they are. Everyone must know your contact's phone number.
- Discuss what to do in an evacuation. Plan how to take care of your pets.

3. Complete this checklist.

- Post emergency numbers next to telephones (fire, police, ambulance, etc.).
- Teach children how and when to call 911 or your local Emergency Medical Services number for emergency help.
- Show each family member how and when to turn off the utilities (water, gas, and electricity) at the main switches.
- Check that you have adequate insurance coverage.
- Get training from the fire department for each family member on how to use the fire extinguisher (ABC type). Make sure that they know where it's kept.
- Install smoke detectors on each floor, especially near bedrooms.
- Stock emergency supplies and assemble a Disaster Supplies Kit.
- Take a Red Cross first aid and CPR class.
- Determine escape routes from your home. Find two ways to get out of each room.
- Find the safe places in your home for each type of disaster.

4. Practice and maintain your plan.

- Quiz your children every six months or so.
- Conduct fire and emergency evacuations.
- Replace stored water and food every six months.
- Test and recharge fire extinguishers according to the manufacturer's instructions.
- Test smoke detectors monthly and change the batteries at least once a year.

Neighbors helping neighbors

Working with neighbors can save lives and protect property. Meet with your neighbors to plan how the neighborhood could work together after a disaster until help arrives. If you're a member of a neighborhood organization, like a home association or crime watch group, introduce disaster preparedness as a new activity. Know your neighbors' special skills (e.g., medical, technical) and consider how you could help neighbors who have special needs, like disabled and

elderly persons. Make plans for child care in case parents can't get home.
    If disaster strikes:

- Remain calm and patient. Put your plan into action.
- Check for injuries.
- Give first aid and get help for seriously injured people.
- Listen to your battery-powered radio for news and instructions.
- Check for damage in your home.
- Use flashlights. Do not light matches or turn on electrical switches, if you suspect damage.
- Sniff for gas leaks, starting at a gas water heater. If you smell gas or suspect a leak, turn off the main gas valve, open windows, and get everyone outside quickly.
- Shut off any other damaged utilities. (You will need a professional to turn the gas back on.)
- Clean up spilled medicines, bleaches, gasoline, and other flammable liquids immediately.
- Remember to confine or secure your pets.
- Call your family contact—do not use the telephone again unless it is a life-threatening emergency.
- Check on your neighbors, especially elderly or disabled persons.
- Make sure you have an adequate water supply in case service is cut off.
- Stay away from downed power lines.
- To get copies of American Red Cross community disaster education materials, contact your local Red Cross chapter.

Disaster Supplies Kit

SOURCES: American Red Cross and FEMA
    There are six basics you should stock for your home: water, food, first aid supplies, clothing and bedding, tools and emergency supplies, and special items. Keep the items that you would most likely need during an evacuation in an easy-to carry container. Possible containers include a large, covered trash container, a camping backpack, or a duffle bag.

Water

Store water in plastic containers such as soft drink bottles. Avoid using containers that will decompose or break, like milk cartons or glass bottles. A normally active person needs to drink at least two quarts of water each day. Hot environments and intense physical activity can double that amount. Children, nursing mothers, and ill people will need more water.

- Store one gallon of water per person per day.
- Keep at least a three-day supply of water per person (two quarts for drinking, two quarts for each person in your household for food preparation and sanitation).

Food

Store at least a three-day supply of non-perishable food. Select foods that require no refrigeration, preparation, or cooking, and little or no water. If you must heat food, buy a can of sterno. Select food items that are compact and lightweight. Include a selection of the following foods in your Disaster Supplies Kit:

- Ready-to-eat canned meats, fruits, and vegetables
- Canned juices
- Staples (salt, sugar, pepper, spices, etc.)
- High energy foods
- Vitamins
- Food for infants
- Comfort/stress foods (sweets)

First Aid Kit

Assemble a first aid kit for your home and one for each car.

- Sterile adhesive bandages in assorted sizes
- Assorted sizes of safety pins
- Cleansing agent or soap
- Latex gloves (2 pairs)
- Sunscreen
- 2-inch sterile gauze pads (4-6)
- 4-inch sterile gauze pads (4-6)

- Triangular bandages (3)
- Non-prescription drugs (see below)
- 2-inch sterile rolled bandages (3 rolls)
- 3-inch sterile rolled bandages (3 rolls)
- Scissors
- Tweezers
- Needle
- Moistened towelettes
- Antiseptic
- Thermometer
- Tongue depressors (2)
- Tube of petroleum jelly or other lubricant

Non-Prescription Drugs

- Aspirin or non-aspirin pain reliever
- Anti-diarrhea medication
- Antacid (for stomach upset)
- Laxative
- Activated charcoal (use if advised to do so by the Poison Control Center)

Tools and Supplies

- Mess kits, or paper cups, plates, and plastic utensils
- Emergency preparedness manual
- Battery-operated radio and extra batteries
- Flashlight and extra batteries
- Cash or traveler's checks, coins
- Non-electric can opener, utility knife
- Fire extinguisher: small canister ABC type
- Tube tent
- Pliers
- Tape

- Compass
- Matches in a waterproof container
- Aluminum foil
- Plastic storage containers
- Signal flare
- Paper, pencil
- Needles, thread
- Medicine dropper
- Shut-off wrench, to turn off household gas and water
- Whistle
- Plastic sheeting
- Map of the area (for locating shelters)

Sanitation

- Toilet paper, towelettes
- Soap, liquid detergent
- Feminine supplies
- Personal hygiene items
- Plastic garbage bags, ties (for personal sanitation use)
- Plastic bucket with tight lid
- Disinfectant
- Household chlorine bleach

Clothing and Bedding

- Sturdy shoes or work boots
- Rain gear
- Blankets or sleeping bags
- Hat and gloves
- Thermal underwear
- Sunglasses

Special Items

Remember family members with special requirements, such as infants and elderly or disabled persons

For Baby

- Formula
- Diapers
- Bottles
- Powdered milk
- Medications

For Adults

- Heart and high blood pressure medication
- Insulin
- Other prescription drugs
- Denture needs
- Contact lenses and supplies
- Extra eyeglasses

Entertainment

- Games and books

Important Family Documents

Keep these records in a waterproof, portable container:

- Will, insurance policies, contracts deeds, stocks and bonds
- Passports, social security cards, immunization records

- Bank account numbers
- Credit card account numbers and companies
- Inventory of valuable household goods, important telephone numbers
- Family records (birth, marriage, death certificates)

Store your kit in a convenient place known to all family members. Keep a smaller version of the supplies kit in the trunk of your car.

Keep items in airtight plastic bags. Change your stored water supply every six months so that it stays fresh. Replace your stored food every six months. Re-evaluate your kit and family needs at least once a year. Replace batteries, update clothing, etc.

Ask your physician or pharmacist about storing prescription medications.

General Disaster Preparedness Materials: Children & Disasters

"Disaster Preparedness Coloring Book" (ARC 2200, English, or ARC 2200S, Spanish) Children & Disasters ages 3-10.

"Adventures of the Disaster Dudes" (ARC 5024) video and Presenter's Guide for use by an adult with children in grades 4-6.

To get copies of American Red Cross Community Disaster Education materials, contact your local Red Cross chapter.

Motivation

Motivation

Other Meeting Topics

The first meeting with your group is only the beginning. Meeting together on a regular basis to receive training on other topics allows participants to become better acquainted with each other. It also educates the neighborhood about other subjects that may be a concern to the group. Take advantage of the resources available to make your neighborhood a safer place to live.

The Crime Prevention Presentation Outline identifies a number of other potential topics for Block Group meetings (see page 42). Although local law enforcement will probably be the primary resource for much of this training, there are many other resources that are available to your Block Group. Here are just a few for your consideration: Federal Bureau of Investigation, Drug Enforcement Administration, U.S. Postal Inspection Service or your local Postmaster, Department of Homeland Security, Federal Emergency Management Agency, State Police, Attorney General's Office, consumer affairs organizations, mental health agencies, senior agencies, security firms, insurance agents, the Red Cross, United Way, farm bureaus, and professional and trade associations.

If you would like more information about any of these crime prevention or training programs, please contact your Community Watch Program or District Coordinator to learn more.

Sign Posting

Having a Community Watch sign without an active Block Group becomes ineffective when criminals realize that the group isn't doing anything. For that reason, many communities have guidelines for issuing and maintaining block signs. If your Block Group becomes inactive, you could lose the privilege of having a sign posted!

If you want a sign in your block, you will need to find out what the requirements are for your community. Talk with your District or Program Coordinator to find out.

One of the requirements used in some Community Watch programs is completion of the Crime Survey. A sign will not be issued until a certain percentage (50 percent, for example) of residents have completed the survey. Another requirement may be consistent Block Group meetings. They need to be held on a regular basis and achieve a specified level of attendance. Some Community Watch Programs remove signs when Block Groups become inactive, so you'll want to check into this as well. Your Program or District Coordinator can spell out what you need to do to qualify for Community Watch signs.

Once you know the criteria, you will probably need to complete an application for the sign. Feel free to use or adapt the generic sign application form in the back of this handbook.

Before erecting any signs, be sure you know the regulations in your town or county. Determine the maximum height that the signs can be placed, and the placement of signs on street lights, utility poles, and traffic lights. Many communities restrict sign placement. Also determine whether signs can be posted on a pole placed in a yard. Be sure to place signs at the entrance points of your neighborhood.

Researching and erecting signs is a great assignment to give a volunteer on your block. By doing so, you begin to share the work of the Block Group, and your neighbors will begin to realize that their Block Group is a joint responsibility.

Maintaining Your Watch Group

We call this program Community Watch for a reason. Remaining flexible and addressing the needs of the community in *all* areas maintains growth and enthusiasm. It allows you to appeal to just about everyone at some level. Some people care very much about crime prevention. Others care about traffic and safety issues. Others have concerns about taxes, healthcare, or other topics.

Therefore, one of the most important things you ever do as a Block Captain will be to find out what folks on your block care about and make sure that the management team and Steering Committee know about it. If you can help your Block Group members achieve their goals, their commitment to the program will grow and maintaining the group will be easier.

As Block Captain, you can also encourage creative thinking about how to get things done. Be on the lookout for special projects that can get people involved and build their enthusiasm. One possibility is to have a contest. The following are some ideas to consider.

In the spring or summer, hold a contest for the best-landscaped yard. One aspect of the judging could be for design including home security. Use meetings to train residents on how bushes and shrubbery can be shaped to limit hiding places. Talk about lighting issues, too. But don't feel you have to just focus on the crime prevention aspects; go ahead and get an expert to talk about roses and daffodils, Japanese gardens, and the other topics that appeal to most homeowners. Then include all of the features in the judging. See if you can get a local landscape supply store to donate prizes.

In the winter, contests with a Christmas or Hanukkah theme are popular. Base awards on the most creative, innovative, and original design of holiday lighting and decorations. Your block can challenge participants in a neighboring Block Group. Announce the contest in the Community Watch newsletter and local media. This can generate interest and lead to a community-wide event.

Undoubtedly, you and your Block Group members can generate other contest ideas. Have a brainstorming session at your next meeting.

Other Ideas to Motivate Block Groups

Long-time Community and Neighborhood Watch leaders say that social interaction holds groups together. Neighborhoods with people who care about each other and socialize with each other experience fewer crimes and less turnover. The following are some ideas to help you maintain the cohesiveness and enthusiasm of your Block Group.

Sign Posting Celebration - Celebrate the first group achievement by getting together to post the signs received for establishing a watch group. Have a picnic or potluck.

Recycling - Work as a group to recycle products and raise money for the watch group—or for items that benefit the entire neighborhood.

Group Material Purchasing - Some businesses give discounts on large orders. Get together to make purchases of building material, plants and gardening supplies or whatever.

Neighborhood Associations - Are there neighborhood associations in your community? Send a delegate from your block. Residents can rotate attendance and your block can have input in the planning and policymaking for your area.

Emergency Planning - Your block can get together to plan what to do in an emergency. Take inventory of special skills and equipment in case of emergencies. *Note*: This is an excellent project for group buying, because everyone can benefit from stocking up on emergency supplies.

Telephone Reassurance and Visits - A schedule to check on the elderly and people who are confined to their homes can be made to ensure everything is all right with them.

Work Parties - If residents have similar needs such as painting, gardening, housecleaning, shoveling snow, etc;, these tasks are accomplished faster and easier when a group does them together.

Holiday Activities - A community center or neighborhood church may donate space for a Block Group dinner. Decorating homes or the entire block can be done together.

Progressive Dinners - Portions of the meal are served at each house on the block and all of the participants go from house to house until the meal is finished. Soup may be served at one house, then salad at another, then the main course at another, and so on.

Carpooling - Share rides to work, to shopping centers, to pick up groceries, wherever and whenever possible.

Block Gardens - Either a space common to all of the residents or an unused piece of land at someone's home can provide the space for a community garden. A harvest celebration can be held at the end of the growing season.

Exercise Groups - Walking together or joining an aerobic class with other neighbors can make exercise easier and more fun.

Goods and Services Exchange - Unwanted books, clothing, toys, etc., can be collected and exchanged between neighbors. Also find out what talents neighbors have and share them with each other. Skills in gardening, auto repair, carpentry, art, and music can be shared and enjoyed by all. These talents could be exhibited at picnics and other get-togethers.

Group Garage Sale - This can be one big garage sale where everyone brings merchandise to a single location or a series of garage sales held on the same day throughout the neighborhood.

Block Parties - These kinds of get-togethers promote communication and relationships with neighbors. This increases the cohesion of the group.

Anything you can think of that brings the neighborhood together is a good idea. Do not be afraid to offer and invite suggestions. The group can only benefit from becoming more involved with each other.

Appendix

Appendix

Community Watch Forms

The great thing about Community Watch is that it gives you a ready-to-implement system easily adaptable to the needs of your own community. To help you get off and running, we have created a set of convenient forms that will help you in everything from recruiting volunteers to running meetings.

This appendix includes all of the forms referred to in *Block Captain's Handbook*. As with everything else in this handbook, you are welcome to use the information contained here to create your own forms. You may even photocopy them (enlarge by 120% for best results). Or, to save you time, Crime Prevention Resources can furnish you with a complete supply of forms to get you started (for a modest fee).

To place your order, or for further information, contact us at:

Crime Prevention Resources
33 N. Central, Ste. 219
Medford, OR 97501
Telephone: 1-800-867-0016
Fax: 1-541-772-8239
E-mail: tmonson@advantagesource.com
Website: www.crimeprevent.com

List of Forms

Citizens Crime Survey

Citizens Crime Survey Tabulation

Volunteer Application

Volunteer Reference Follow Up Form

Newsletter Mastheads

Newsletter Layout

Meeting Announcement Flyer

Meeting Announcement Postcard

Meeting Announcement Doorhanger

Meeting Sign-In Sheet

Member Profile Form

Block Map-Traditional

Block Map-Cul-de-Sac

Block Map-Apartment

Telephone Tree Form

Sign Application Form

Watch Family Information Form

Home Security Survey

Household Inventory

Suspicious Activity/Crime Report

Citizen Crime Survey
NUMBER OF REPORTED CRIMES

Thinking about the neighborhood in which you live, have you or has any member of your family living with you been a victim of any of the crimes listed (or any other crimes not listed) in your neighborhood?

Please record the number of crimes reported to law enforcement.

	PAST 6 MONTHS	PAST 12 MONTHS
Crimes Against Property		
Burglary (Items stolen from your home)	_____	_____
Fraud (Theft by deception)	_____	_____
Theft (Auto or property not in the home)	_____	_____
Vandalism (Property destroyed)	_____	_____
Other (Please specify)	_____	_____
Crimes Against a Person		
Assault/Battery (Physical violence or threat)	_____	_____
Robbery (With violence or threat of violence)	_____	_____
Sexual Assault (Rape or attempted rape)	_____	_____
Other (Please specify)	_____	_____

TOTAL DOLLAR VALUE OF LOST PROPERTY _____

(If stolen property was recovered, do not include.)

Citizen Crime Survey

NUMBER OF UNREPORTED CRIMES

Please record the number of crimes NOT reported to law enforcement.

	PAST 6 MONTHS	PAST 12 MONTHS
Crimes Against Property		
Burglary (Items stolen from your home)	_____	_____
Fraud (Theft by deception)	_____	_____
Theft (Auto or property not in the home)	_____	_____
Vandalism (Property destroyed)	_____	_____
Other (Please specify)	_____	_____
Crimes Against a Person		
Assault/Battery (Physical violence or threat)	_____	_____
Robbery (With violence or threat of violence)	_____	_____
Sexual Assault (Rape or attempted rape)	_____	_____
Other (Please specify)	_____	_____

TOTAL DOLLAR VALUE OF LOST PROPERTY _____

(If stolen property was recovered, do not include.)

Citizen Crime Survey

CRIME PERCEPTION SURVEY

Thinking about crimes committed in your neighborhood during the last year, would you say that:

_____Crime has increased

_____Crime is about the same

_____Crime has decreased a little

_____Crime has decreased a lot

_____Don't know

_____No answer

Thinking about walking down the street on which you live, how safe do you feel walking DURING THE DAY? Please rate from 1 to 10, 10 being the most safe and 1 being the least safe. (NA = REFUSED OR NO OPINION)

1 2 3 4 5 6 7 8 9 10 NA (circle one)

How safe do you feel walking AT NIGHT? Please rate from 1 to 10, 10 being the most safe and 1 being the least safe. (NA = REFUSED OR NO OPINION)

1 2 3 4 5 6 7 8 9 10 NA (circle one)

Thinking about being inside your home, how safe do you feel at home DURING THE DAY? Please rate from 1 to 10, 10 being the most safe and 1 being the least safe. (NA = REFUSED OR NO OPINION)

1 2 3 4 5 6 7 8 9 10 NA (circle one)

How safe do you feel at home AT NIGHT? Please rate from 1 to 10, 10 being the most safe and 1 being the least safe. (NA = REFUSED OR NO OPINION)

1 2 3 4 5 6 7 8 9 10 NA (circle one)

Thinking about potential crimes against you or your family members, use the scale to rate the crimes listed below: SCALE :1 = most fear, 10 = least fear

Citizen Crime Survey

CRIME PERCEPTION SURVEY (Cont'd)

Thinking about walking down the street on which you live, how safe do you feel walking DURING THE DAY? Please rate from 1 to 10, 10 being the most safe and 1 being the least safe. (NA = REFUSED OR NO OPINION)

Crimes Against Your Property	**Circle one please**
Burglary (Items stolen from your home)	1 2 3 4 5 6 7 8 9 10 NA
Fraud (Theft by deception)	1 2 3 4 5 6 7 8 9 10 NA
Theft (Auto or property not in the home)	1 2 3 4 5 6 7 8 9 10 NA
Vandalism (Property destroyed)	1 2 3 4 5 6 7 8 9 10 NA
Other (Please specify)	1 2 3 4 5 6 7 8 9 10 AN

_____

_____

Crimes Against Your Person	**Circle one please**
Assault/Battery (Violence or threat)	1 2 3 4 5 6 7 8 9 10 NA
Robbery (With violence or threat)	1 2 3 4 5 6 7 8 9 10 NA
Sexual Assault (Rape or attempted rape)	1 2 3 4 5 6 7 8 9 10 NA
Other (Please specify)	1 2 3 4 5 6 7 8 9 10 NA

_____

_____

Citizen Crime Survey Tabulation

SURVEY ADMINISTRATOR: Record total responses on this page.

NUMBER OF REPORTED CRIMES

Please record the number of crimes reported to law enforcement.

	PAST 6 MONTHS	PAST 12 MONTHS
Crimes Against Property		
Burglary (Items stolen from your home)	_____	_____
Fraud (Theft by deception)	_____	_____
Theft (Auto or property not in the home)	_____	_____
Vandalism (Property destroyed)	_____	_____
Other (Please specify)	_____	_____
Crimes Against a Person		
Assault/Battery (Physical violence or threat)	_____	_____
Robbery (With violence or threat of violence)	_____	_____
Sexual Assault (Rape or attempted rape)	_____	_____
Other (Please specify)	_____	_____

TOTAL DOLLAR VALUE OF LOST PROPERTY   _____

Citizen Crime Survey Tabulation

SURVEY ADMINISTRATOR: Record total responses on this page.

NUMBER OF UNREPORTED CRIMES

Please record the number of crimes NOT reported to law enforcement.

	PAST 6 MONTHS	PAST 12 MONTHS
Crimes Against Property		
Burglary (Items stolen from your home)	_____	_____
Fraud (Theft by deception)	_____	_____
Theft (Auto or property not in the home)	_____	_____
Vandalism (Property destroyed)	_____	_____
Other (Please specify)	_____	_____
Crimes Against a Person		
Assault/Battery (Physical violence or threat)	_____	_____
Robbery (With violence or threat of violence)	_____	_____
Sexual Assault (Rape or attempted rape)	_____	_____
Other (Please specify)	_____	_____

TOTAL DOLLAR VALUE OF LOST PROPERTY _____

Citizen Crime Survey Tabulation

SURVEY ADMINISTRATOR: Record total responses on this page.

Thinking about crimes committed in their neighborhood during the last year, respondents would say that:

TOTALS

Crime has increased   _____

Crime is about the same   _____

Crime has decreased a little   _____

Crime has decreased a lot   _____

Don't know   _____

No answer   _____

Citizen Crime Survey Tabulation

SURVEY ADMINISTRATOR: Record total responses on this page.

Walking down their street **DURING THE DAY** how safe they feel.
10 is the most safe and 1 si the least safe.

1	2	3	4	5	6	7	8	9	10	NA
____	____	____	____	____	____	____	____	____	____	_____

Walking down their street **AT NIGHT** how safe they feel.
10 is the most safe and 1 si the least safe.

1	2	3	4	5	6	7	8	9	10	NA
____	____	____	____	____	____	____	____	____	____	_____

At home **DURING THE DAY** how safe they feel.
10 is the most safe and 1 si the least safe.

1	2	3	4	5	6	7	8	9	10	NA
____	____	____	____	____	____	____	____	____	____	_____

At home **AT NIGHT** how safe they feel.
10 is the most safe and 1 si the least safe.

1	2	3	4	5	6	7	8	9	10	NA
____	____	____	____	____	____	____	____	____	____	_____

BURGLARY

SCALE: 1 = most fear, 10 = least fear

1	2	3	4	5	6	7	8	9	10	NA
____	____	____	____	____	____	____	____	____	____	_____

Citizen Crime Survey Tabulation

SURVEY ADMINISTRATOR: Record total responses on this page.

FRAUD
SCALE: 1 = most fear, 10 = least fear

1	2	3	4	5	6	7	8	9	10	NA
____	____	____	____	____	____	____	____	____	____	_____

THEFT
SCALE: 1 = most fear, 10 = least fear

1	2	3	4	5	6	7	8	9	10	NA
____	____	____	____	____	____	____	____	____	____	_____

VANDALISM

SCALE: 1 = most fear, 10 = least fear

1	2	3	4	5	6	7	8	9	10	NA
____	____	____	____	____	____	____	____	____	____	_____

OTHER PROPERTY CRIME
SCALE: 1 = most fear, 10 = least fear

1	2	3	4	5	6	7	8	9	10	NA
____	____	____	____	____	____	____	____	____	____	_____

ASSAULT/BATTERY
SCALE: 1 = most fear, 10 = least fear

1	2	3	4	5	6	7	8	9	10	NA
____	____	____	____	____	____	____	____	____	____	_____

Citizen Crime Survey Tabulation

SURVEY ADMINISTRATOR: Record total responses on this page.

ROBBERY

SCALE: 1 = most fear, 10 = least fear

1	2	3	4	5	6	7	8	9	10	NA
____	____	____	____	____	____	____	____	____	____	_____

SEXUAL ASSAULT

SCALE: 1 = most fear, 10 = least fear

1	2	3	4	5	6	7	8	9	10	NA
____	____	____	____	____	____	____	____	____	____	_____

OTHER PERSONAL CRIME

SCALE: 1 = most fear, 10 = least fear

1	2	3	4	5	6	7	8	9	10	NA
____	____	____	____	____	____	____	____	____	____	_____

VOLUNTEER APPLICATION

Community **WATCH**

FULL NAME_____
                    LAST   FIRST   MIDDLE

PRESENT ADDRESS_____
                    STREET   CITY   STATE   ZIP

_____
   PHONE NUMBER   SOCIAL SECURITY NUMBER   DRIVER'S LICENSE NUMBER / STATE

ARE YOU EMPLOYED?   ☐ YES   ☐ NO

EMPLOYMENT HISTORY - PAST 10 YEARS

EMPLOYER, PRESENT_____

DUTIES/JOB DESCRIPTION_____

ADDRESS_____

PHONE_____ SUPERVISOR_____

EMPLOYER, PAST_____

DUTIES/JOB DESCRIPTION_____

ADDRESS_____

PHONE_____ SUPERVISOR_____

EMPLOYER, PAST_____

DUTIES/JOB DESCRIPTION_____

ADDRESS_____

PHONE_____ SUPERVISOR_____

MAY WE CONTACT THE EMPLOYERS LISTED ABOVE?   ☐ YES   ☐ NO

EDUCATION

HIGH SCHOOL_____ DID YOU GRADUATE?   ☐ YES   ☐ NO

DID YOU ATTEND COLLEGE?   ☐ YES   ☐ NO

NAME OF COLLEGE_____ YRS COMPLETED_____

MAJOR COURSE OF STUDY_____

VOCATIONAL SCHOOLING? (INCLUDING MILITARY)   ☐ YES   ☐ NO

IF YES, WHAT TYPE OF TRAINING?_____

ANY SPECIAL SKILLS? (COMPUTERS, CONSULTING, ETC.)_____

COMPLETELY ANSWER ALL QUESTIONS - IF NECESSARY, USE ADDITIONAL SHEETS OF PAPER.

PERSONAL REFERENCES

1. NAME_____

ADDRESS_____

HOW LONG KNOWN_____ PHONE NUMBER_____

2. NAME_____

ADDRESS_____

HOW LONG KNOWN_____ PHONE NUMBER_____

3. NAME_____

ADDRESS_____

HOW LONG KNOWN_____ PHONE NUMBER_____

* DO YOU KNOW ANYONE THAT WORKS FOR THIS DEPARTMENT?   □ YES   □ NO

IF YES, THEIR NAME_____

In the space below, briefly describe why you want to volunteer and what you would like to gain from the

experience:_____

_____

_____

How long would you like to volunteer each week?_____

Have you ever worked with law enforcement before?   □ YES   □ NO

If yes, in what capacity?_____

Have you ever been convicted of a felony?   □ YES   □ NO

If yes, give date(s) and nature of offense(s)_____

_____

_____

I understand that a background check is required prior to possible assignment as a volunteer and that due to the sensitive nature of some positions, the results of the background check may require this department to not allow me to fill said positions.

I also understand that this department will do everything in its power to try to find a position that will suit my needs and the needs of the department and that the needs of the department must come first in determining my selected positions.

I certify that the information I have given on this application is true and correct to the best of my knowledge and understand that falsification of this information is grounds for dismissal. Permission, unless indicated to the contrary, is granted to confirm by personal inquiry or such other necessary means the information set forth herein. Any information so obtained shall remain confidential.

Applicant's Signature_____ Date_____

VOLUNTEER REFERENCE
FOLLOW UP FORM

Community **WATCH**

Use this sheet to record the interviews with the references listed on the Volunteer Application.
Use the questions listed here and if necessary add your own questions.

APPLICANT'S NAME_____

POSITION APPLIED FOR_____

Reference's Name - How do you know the applicant?

1._____ - _____

2._____ - _____

3._____ - _____

How long have you known the applicant?

1._____ 2._____ 3._____

On a scale of 1 to 10, how would you rate the applicant on the following characteristics?

Ability to work with people?

1._____ 2._____ 3._____

Ability to communicate?

1._____ 2._____ 3._____

Integrity?

1._____ 2._____ 3._____

As a self starter?

1._____ 2._____ 3._____

Perseverance?

1._____ 2._____ 3._____

What do you feel his or her strengths are?

1a._____ 2a._____ 3a._____

1b._____ 2b._____ 3b._____

If a past employer - Would you hire him or her back?

1._____ 2._____ 3._____

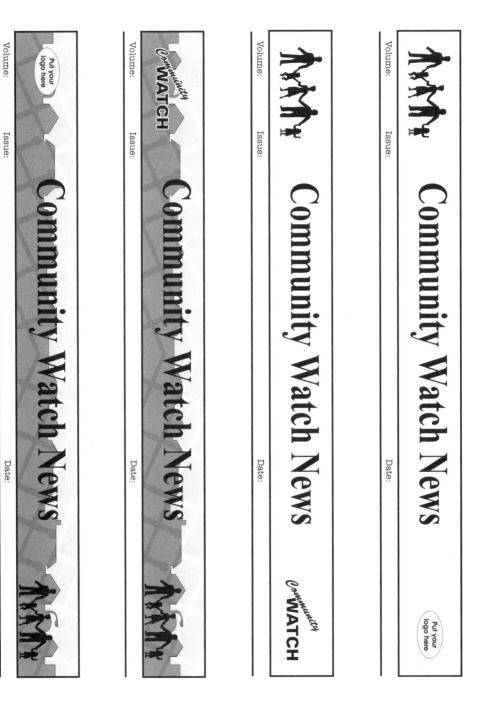

Community Watch News

Volume: Issue: Date:

Community Watch News

Volume: Issue: Date:

Community Watch News

Volume: Issue: Date:

Community Watch News

Volume: Issue: Date:

Community Watch News

Volume:	Issue:	Date:

Inside this issue:

WATCH

How safe is our community?

**We are having a short meeting to discuss how
we can protect ourselves and our families.
Please join us!**

DATE:_____

TIME:_____

LOCATION:_____

HOSTED BY:_____

PHONE:_____

How your participation helps you and others:

* Gain an opportunity to voice your concerns

   about problems or situations you have seen.

* Reduce crime in our community.

* Provide a safer neighborhood for you and

   your family.

COPYRIGHT 1992, 2003 CRIME PREVENTION RESOURCES

Community **WATCH**

Is our neighborhood safe?

Your neighbors are having a short meeting to discuss several ways we can make our homes and community a safer place to live and work.

Please join us!

DATE:_____

TIME:_____

LOCATION:_____

HOSTED BY:_____ PHONE:_____

At this meeting we will discuss the things we all can do to ensure that our homes and our neighborhood are a safe place to live. On behalf of your neighbors and your law enforcement officials, we look forward to seeing you there.

Is our neighborhood safe?

Your neighbors are having a short meeting to discuss several ways we can make our homes and community a safer place to live and work.

Please join us!

DATE:_____

TIME:_____

LOCATION:_____

HOSTED BY:_____ PHONE:_____

At this meeting we will discuss the things we all can do to ensure that our homes and our neighborhood are a safe place to live. On behalf of your neighbors and your law enforcement officials, we look forward to seeing you there.

Is our neighborhood safe?

Your neighbors are having a short meeting to discuss several ways we make our homes and our community a safer place to live and work.

You are invited to join us!

DATE:_____

TIME:_____

LOCATION:_____

HOSTED BY:_____

PHONE:_____

At this meeting we will discuss the things we all can do to ensure that our homes and our neighborhood are a safe place to live. On behalf of your neighbors and your law enforcement officials, we look forward to seeing you there.

Community **WATCH**

Community WATCH — MEETING SIGN IN SHEET

PLEASE SIGN IN BELOW (PRINT CLEARLY)

NAME	ADDRESS	PHONE NO.

Community **WATCH**

BLOCK PROFILE SHEET
MEMBER PROFILES

NUMBER / STREET COLOR OF HOUSE	NAMES & AGES OF RESIDENTS	TELEPHONE / EMAIL HOME - WORK EMERGENCY	AUTOS: MAKE / MODEL / COLOR / LICENSE NUMBER	SECURITY SURVEY COMPLETE?	OPERATION ID COMPLETE?	ALARM INSTALLED?	MEDICAL PROBLEMS? NAME / PROBLEM	SPECIAL TRAINING OR SKILLS?

BLOCK MAP - Traditional

Indicate **NORTH** with arrow

NAME
ADDRESS / COLOR
HOME PHONE
WORK PHONE

NAME
ADDRESS / COLOR
HOME PHONE
WORK PHONE

STREET NAME

STREET NAME

NAME
ADDRESS / COLOR
HOME PHONE
WORK PHONE

NAME
ADDRESS / COLOR
HOME PHONE
WORK PHONE

NAME
ADDRESS / COLOR
HOME PHONE
WORK PHONE

NAME
ADDRESS / COLOR
HOME PHONE
WORK PHONE

NAME
ADDRESS / COLOR
HOME PHONE
WORK PHONE

NAME
ADDRESS / COLOR
HOME PHONE
WORK PHONE

NAME
ADDRESS / COLOR
HOME PHONE
WORK PHONE

NAME
ADDRESS / COLOR
HOME PHONE
WORK PHONE

NAME
ADDRESS / COLOR
HOME PHONE
WORK PHONE

NAME
ADDRESS / COLOR
HOME PHONE
WORK PHONE

NAME
ADDRESS / COLOR
HOME PHONE
WORK PHONE

NAME
ADDRESS / COLOR
HOME PHONE
WORK PHONE

Community **WATCH**

COPYRIGHT 1992, 2003 CRIME PREVENTION RESOURCES

BLOCK MAP - Cul-de-Sac

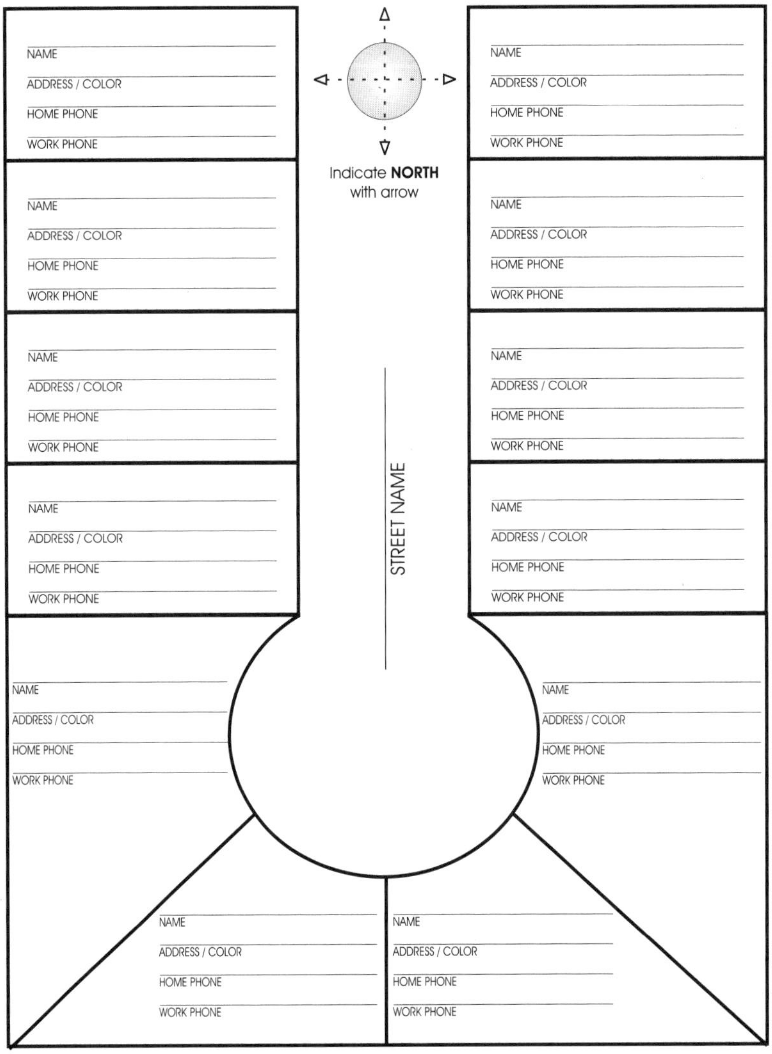

NAME
ADDRESS / COLOR
HOME PHONE
WORK PHONE

NAME
ADDRESS / COLOR
HOME PHONE
WORK PHONE

NAME
ADDRESS / COLOR
HOME PHONE
WORK PHONE

NAME
ADDRESS / COLOR
HOME PHONE
WORK PHONE

Indicate **NORTH**
with arrow

NAME
ADDRESS / COLOR
HOME PHONE
WORK PHONE

NAME
ADDRESS / COLOR
HOME PHONE
WORK PHONE

NAME
ADDRESS / COLOR
HOME PHONE
WORK PHONE

NAME
ADDRESS / COLOR
HOME PHONE
WORK PHONE

STREET NAME

NAME
ADDRESS / COLOR
HOME PHONE
WORK PHONE

NAME
ADDRESS / COLOR
HOME PHONE
WORK PHONE

NAME
ADDRESS / COLOR
HOME PHONE
WORK PHONE

NAME
ADDRESS / COLOR
HOME PHONE
WORK PHONE

Community **WATCH**

COPYRIGHT 1992, 2003 CRIME PREVENTION RESOURCES

APARTMENT/HOUSING MAP

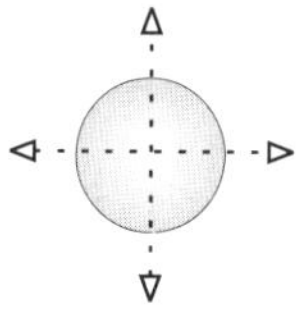

Indicate **NORTH** with arrow

HALLWAY LEVEL

NAME	NAME
APT. NUMBER	APT. NUMBER
HOME PHONE	HOME PHONE
WORK PHONE	WORK PHONE
NAME	NAME
APT. NUMBER	APT. NUMBER
HOME PHONE	HOME PHONE
WORK PHONE	WORK PHONE
NAME	NAME
APT. NUMBER	APT. NUMBER
HOME PHONE	HOME PHONE
WORK PHONE	WORK PHONE
NAME	NAME
APT. NUMBER	APT. NUMBER
HOME PHONE	HOME PHONE
WORK PHONE	WORK PHONE
NAME	NAME
APT. NUMBER	APT. NUMBER
HOME PHONE	HOME PHONE
WORK PHONE	WORK PHONE
NAME	NAME
APT. NUMBER	APT. NUMBER
HOME PHONE	HOME PHONE
WORK PHONE	WORK PHONE
NAME	NAME
APT. NUMBER	APT. NUMBER
HOME PHONE	HOME PHONE
WORK PHONE	WORK PHONE

Community **WATCH**

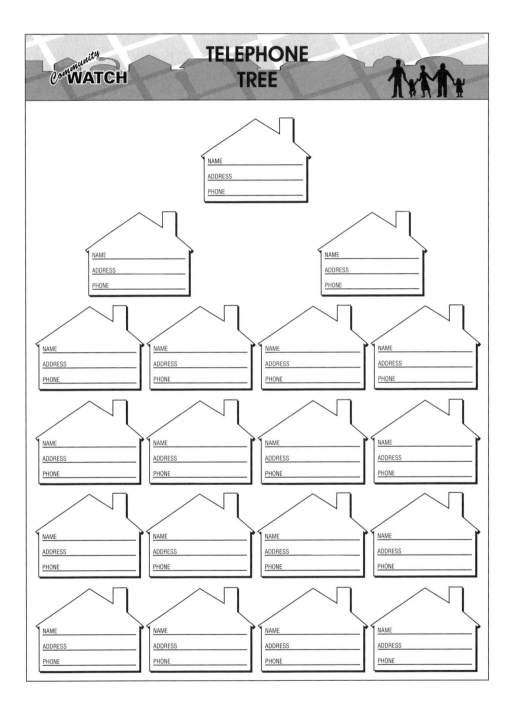

Community WATCH

SIGN APPLICATION

BLOCK CAPTAIN'S NAME: *(LAST NAME, FIRST NAME)*

GROUP NUMBER:

BLOCK CAPTAIN'S ADDRESS:

HOME PHONE:

DATE OF FIRST MEETING:

WORK PHONE:

DATE OF NEXT MEETING:

EMAIL:

NAME	ADDRESS	HOME SURVEY	DOORS & WINDOWS SECURE	OPERATION ID	HOUSE NUMBERS FRNT/BCK	BUSHES & SHRUBS TRIMMED	EXTERIOR & PORCH LIGHTS

Watch Family Information

Community WATCH

Address:_____ Telephone:_____

_____ Email:_____

NAMES:

Adult Male:_____ Adult Female:_____

Child 1:_____ Age:_____ Child 4:_____ Age:_____

Child 2:_____ Age:_____ Child 5:_____ Age:_____

Child 3:_____ Age:_____ Child 6:_____ Age:_____

Other Occupants:_____

IN CASE OF EMERGENCY CONTACT:

Name:_____ Telephone - Home:_____

Address:_____ Telephone - Work:_____

VEHICLES:

Owner	Year	Make	Body Style	Color	License No.
1.					
2.					
3.					

Medical or health problems/name:_____

_____

Medical training or skills:_____

_____

Other information/comments:_____

_____

HOME SECURITY SURVEY

Take a few minutes to follow this list of recommendations to help secure your house. By checking off each item on the list you will significantly reduce the chances that you will be one of the millions of homes that are broken into each year.

FRONT YARD

☐ Street numbers easily visible from street. Critical time can be saved by emergency vehicles when the street address of the house is clearly visible from a distance.

☐ Bushes, shrubs and trees are pruned away from windows and doors. Burglars and thieves are less likely to break into a window or door when there is a chance to be seen.

☐ Bushes, shrubs and trees are pruned to eliminate other potential hiding places. A residence offering limited potential hiding places is less attractive to a burglar.

☐ Limited or directed access to yard. A fence with gates or shrubs at the front of the yard will create a physical and mental barrier that burglars will be less likely to cross.

☐ Locks on gates, where applicable. The ease of entrance to the yard is additionally reduced by locking out potential intruders.

☐ Lighting covers the entire front of house and all hiding places. Well-lit houses are less likely to be burglarized.

Comments:

LEFT SIDE YARD

☐ Lighting adequately covers each entrance
☐ Bushes, shrubs and trees are pruned
☐ Fence is secure

BACK YARD

☐ Lighting adequately covers each entrance.
☐ Bushes, shrubs and trees are pruned
☐ Fence is secure

RIGHT SIDE YARD

☐ Lighting adequately covers each entrance
☐ Bushes, shrubs and trees are pruned
☐ Fence is secure

OUTBUILDINGS

(Detached garage, storage sheds & barns)
☐ Locks on all doors
☐ Locks on all windows
☐ Lighting on entrances

GARAGE DOOR
☐ Internal lock
☐ External lock with hasp
☐ Hinges secure

LIVING ROOM

FRONT ENTRANCE DOOR
☐ Door construction   solid core   metal clad
☐ Dead bolt with minimum 1" throw
☐ Strike plates
☐ Door jambs secure
☐ Molding tight and secure
☐ Hinge pins on inside or otherwise secure
☐ Viewer or window in door
☐ Warning sticker clearly visible
☐ For double doors, stationary door secured
WINDOWS: ☐ SLIDER ☐ DOUBLE HUNG
☐ CRANK ☐ LOUVER
☐ Security device in place (pin or lock)
Comments:

FAMILY ROOM

Door to exterior:
PATIO DOOR
☐ Anti-slide device "Charlie Bar" or dowel
☐ Anti-lift device pin or screws in track
☐ Warning sticker clearly visible
HINGED DOOR
☐ Door construction solid core metal clad
☐ Dead bolt with minimum 1" throw
☐ Strike plates
☐ Door jambs secure
☐ Molding tight and secure
☐ Hinge pins on inside or otherwise secure
☐ Viewer or window in door
☐ Warning sticker clearly visible
☐ For double doors, stationary door secured
WINDOWS:
☐ SLIDER ☐ DOUBLE HUNG ☐ CRANK
☐ LOUVER
☐ Security device in place (pin or lock)
Comments:

HOME SECURITY SURVEY

KITCHEN/UTILITY ROOM

Door to exterior:

__PATIO DOOR__
- ☐ Anti-slide device "Charlie Bar" or dowel
- ☐ Anti-lift device pin or screws in track
- ☐ Warning sticker clearly visible

__HINGED DOOR__
- ☐ Door construction solid core metal clad
- ☐ Dead bolt with minimum 1" throw
- ☐ Strike plates
- ☐ Door jambs secure
- ☐ Molding tight and secure
- ☐ Hinge pins on inside or otherwise secure
- ☐ Viewer or window in door
- ☐ Warning sticker clearly visible
- ☐ For double doors, stationary door secured

__WINDOWS:__ ☐ SLIDER ☐ DOUBLE HUNG
☐ CRANK ☐ LOUVER
- ☐ Security device in place (pin or lock)

Comments:

BEDROOM NO. 1.

__WINDOWS:__ ☐ SLIDER ☐ DOUBLE HUNG
☐ CRANK ☐ LOUVER
- ☐ Security device in place (pin or lock)

Comments:

BEDROOM NO. 2

__WINDOWS:__ ☐ SLIDER ☐ DOUBLE HUNG
☐ CRANK ☐ LOUVER
- ☐ Security device in place (pin or lock)

Comments:

BEDROOM NO. 3

__WINDOWS:__ ☐ SLIDER ☐ DOUBLE HUNG
☐ CRANK ☐ LOUVER
- ☐ Security device in place (pin or lock)

Comments:

BEDROOM NO. 4/DEN

__WINDOWS:__ ☐ SLIDER ☐ DOUBLE HUNG
☐ CRANK ☐ LOUVER
- ☐ Security device in place (pin or lock)

Comments:

BATHROOM NO.1

__WINDOWS:__ ☐ SLIDER ☐ DOUBLE HUNG
CRANK ☐ LOUVER
- ☐ Security device in place (pin or lock)

Comments:

BATHROOM NO.2

__WINDOWS:__ ☐ SLIDER ☐ DOUBLE HUNG
☐ CRANK ☐ LOUVER
- ☐ Security device in place (pin or lock)

Comments:

OTHER

__WINDOWS:__ ☐ SLIDER ☐ DOUBLE HUNG
☐ CRANK ☐ LOUVER
- ☐ Security device in place (pin or lock)

Comments:

BASEMENT

__DOOR AND WINDOWS__
- ☐ Security device in place (pin or lock)

Comments:

OTHER/MISCELLANEOUS

- ☐ Skylights secured
- ☐ Automatic timers for lights, radio, & TV
- ☐ Burglar alarm system
- ☐ Emergency numbers by each phone
- ☐ Grill work on high risk windows - such as a window that may be near a lock on a nearby door.
- ☐ Inventory of contents
- ☐ Safe for valuables
- ☐ Valuables marked

__NOTES:_____

_____

_____

_____

_____

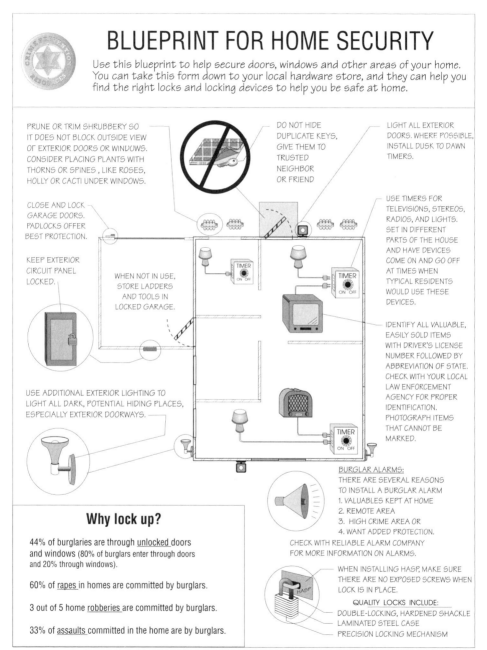

BLUEPRINT FOR HOME SECURITY

Use this blueprint to help secure doors, windows and other areas of your home. You can take this form down to your local hardware store, and they can help you find the right locks and locking devices to help you be safe at home.

PRUNE OR TRIM SHRUBBERY SO IT DOES NOT BLOCK OUTSIDE VIEW OF EXTERIOR DOORS OR WINDOWS. CONSIDER PLACING PLANTS WITH THORNS OR SPINES, LIKE ROSES, HOLLY OR CACTI UNDER WINDOWS.

DO NOT HIDE DUPLICATE KEYS, GIVE THEM TO TRUSTED NEIGHBOR OR FRIEND

LIGHT ALL EXTERIOR DOORS. WHERE POSSIBLE, INSTALL DUSK TO DAWN TIMERS.

CLOSE AND LOCK GARAGE DOORS. PADLOCKS OFFER BEST PROTECTION.

USE TIMERS FOR TELEVISIONS, STEREOS, RADIOS, AND LIGHTS. SET IN DIFFERENT PARTS OF THE HOUSE AND HAVE DEVICES COME ON AND GO OFF AT TIMES WHEN TYPICAL RESIDENTS WOULD USE THESE DEVICES.

KEEP EXTERIOR CIRCUIT PANEL LOCKED.

WHEN NOT IN USE, STORE LADDERS AND TOOLS IN LOCKED GARAGE.

IDENTIFY ALL VALUABLE, EASILY SOLD ITEMS WITH DRIVER'S LICENSE NUMBER FOLLOWED BY ABBREVIATION OF STATE. CHECK WITH YOUR LOCAL LAW ENFORCEMENT AGENCY FOR PROPER IDENTIFICATION. PHOTOGRAPH ITEMS THAT CANNOT BE MARKED.

USE ADDITIONAL EXTERIOR LIGHTING TO LIGHT ALL DARK, POTENTIAL HIDING PLACES, ESPECIALLY EXTERIOR DOORWAYS.

BURGLAR ALARMS:
THERE ARE SEVERAL REASONS TO INSTALL A BURGLAR ALARM
1. VALUABLES KEPT AT HOME
2. REMOTE AREA
3. HIGH CRIME AREA OR
4. WANT ADDED PROTECTION.
CHECK WITH RELIABLE ALARM COMPANY FOR MORE INFORMATION ON ALARMS.

Why lock up?

44% of burglaries are through <u>unlocked</u> doors and windows (80% of burglars enter through doors and 20% through windows).

60% of <u>rapes</u> in homes are committed by burglars.

3 out of 5 home <u>robberies</u> are committed by burglars.

33% of <u>assaults</u> committed in the home are by burglars.

WHEN INSTALLING HASP, MAKE SURE THERE ARE NO EXPOSED SCREWS WHEN LOCK IS IN PLACE.

QUALITY LOCKS INCLUDE:
DOUBLE-LOCKING, HARDENED SHACKLE
LAMINATED STEEL CASE
PRECISION LOCKING MECHANISM

Door and Window Security

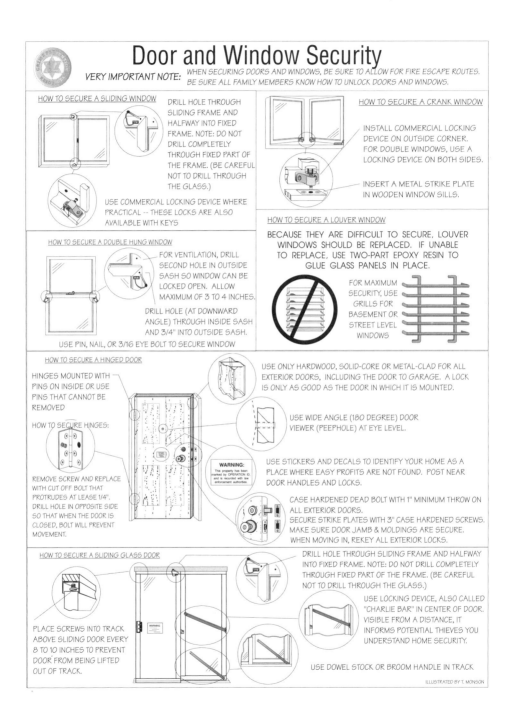

VERY IMPORTANT NOTE: *WHEN SECURING DOORS AND WINDOWS, BE SURE TO ALLOW FOR FIRE ESCAPE ROUTES. BE SURE ALL FAMILY MEMBERS KNOW HOW TO UNLOCK DOORS AND WINDOWS.*

HOW TO SECURE A SLIDING WINDOW

DRILL HOLE THROUGH SLIDING FRAME AND HALFWAY INTO FIXED FRAME. NOTE: DO NOT DRILL COMPLETELY THROUGH FIXED PART OF THE FRAME. (BE CAREFUL NOT TO DRILL THROUGH THE GLASS.)

USE COMMERCIAL LOCKING DEVICE WHERE PRACTICAL -- THESE LOCKS ARE ALSO AVAILABLE WITH KEYS

HOW TO SECURE A CRANK WINDOW

INSTALL COMMERCIAL LOCKING DEVICE ON OUTSIDE CORNER. FOR DOUBLE WINDOWS, USE A LOCKING DEVICE ON BOTH SIDES.

INSERT A METAL STRIKE PLATE IN WOODEN WINDOW SILLS.

HOW TO SECURE A DOUBLE HUNG WINDOW

FOR VENTILATION, DRILL SECOND HOLE IN OUTSIDE SASH SO WINDOW CAN BE LOCKED OPEN. ALLOW MAXIMUM OF 3 TO 4 INCHES.

DRILL HOLE (AT DOWNWARD ANGLE) THROUGH INSIDE SASH AND 3/4" INTO OUTSIDE SASH.

USE PIN, NAIL, OR 3/16 EYE BOLT TO SECURE WINDOW

HOW TO SECURE A LOUVER WINDOW

BECAUSE THEY ARE DIFFICULT TO SECURE, LOUVER WINDOWS SHOULD BE REPLACED. IF UNABLE TO REPLACE, USE TWO-PART EPOXY RESIN TO GLUE GLASS PANELS IN PLACE.

FOR MAXIMUM SECURITY, USE GRILLS FOR BASEMENT OR STREET LEVEL WINDOWS

HOW TO SECURE A HINGED DOOR

HINGES MOUNTED WITH PINS ON INSIDE OR USE PINS THAT CANNOT BE REMOVED

HOW TO SECURE HINGES:

REMOVE SCREW AND REPLACE WITH CUT OFF BOLT THAT PROTRUDES AT LEASE 1/4". DRILL HOLE IN OPPOSITE SIDE SO THAT WHEN THE DOOR IS CLOSED, BOLT WILL PREVENT MOVEMENT.

USE ONLY HARDWOOD, SOLID-CORE OR METAL-CLAD FOR ALL EXTERIOR DOORS, INCLUDING THE DOOR TO GARAGE. A LOCK IS ONLY AS GOOD AS THE DOOR IN WHICH IT IS MOUNTED.

USE WIDE ANGLE (180 DEGREE) DOOR VIEWER (PEEPHOLE) AT EYE LEVEL.

WARNING: This property has been marked by OPERATION ID. and is recorded with law enforcement authorities.

USE STICKERS AND DECALS TO IDENTIFY YOUR HOME AS A PLACE WHERE EASY PROFITS ARE NOT FOUND. POST NEAR DOOR HANDLES AND LOCKS.

CASE HARDENED DEAD BOLT WITH 1" MINIMUM THROW ON ALL EXTERIOR DOORS. SECURE STRIKE PLATES WITH 3" CASE HARDENED SCREWS. MAKE SURE DOOR JAMB & MOLDINGS ARE SECURE. WHEN MOVING IN, REKEY ALL EXTERIOR LOCKS.

HOW TO SECURE A SLIDING GLASS DOOR

DRILL HOLE THROUGH SLIDING FRAME AND HALFWAY INTO FIXED FRAME. NOTE: DO NOT DRILL COMPLETELY THROUGH FIXED PART OF THE FRAME. (BE CAREFUL NOT TO DRILL THROUGH THE GLASS.)

USE LOCKING DEVICE, ALSO CALLED "CHARLIE BAR" IN CENTER OF DOOR. VISIBLE FROM A DISTANCE, IT INFORMS POTENTIAL THIEVES YOU UNDERSTAND HOME SECURITY.

PLACE SCREWS INTO TRACK ABOVE SLIDING DOOR EVERY 8 TO 10 INCHES TO PREVENT DOOR FROM BEING LIFTED OUT OF TRACK.

USE DOWEL STOCK OR BROOM HANDLE IN TRACK

ILLUSTRATED BY T. MONSON

HOUSEHOLD INVENTORY
Protecting the contents of your home

Why is it important to keep an accurate record of your possessions?

It is almost impossible to recreate a list of your personal possessions after a fire or burglary. You constantly collect and buy new items to add to your collection of belongings. And, in the event of a loss, it is nearly impossible to remember all that is lost.

Things like kitchen utensils, clothing, family heirlooms or antiques, valuables and other items lost in a fire or burglary may be forgotten about under the stress of loss. Years after the loss you may remember the brooch Aunt Martha gave you for your twenty-first birthday, or the fishing reel Uncle Fred gave you when you graduated from high school, but by then it is too late to claim them for your insurance or for possible tax deductions.

The only way to be sure to have an accurate record of your possessions is to create an inventory of what you have. An accurate list of everything you own is not only a good idea for fire and theft protection, but in the event you want to divide your property up in a will or present it to other family members as gifts, there will be an accurate list of your possessions.

Video taping and taking photographs add assurance that you have a complete record to quickly check to see what is missing in the event of a fire or burglary. Videos and photographs can speed up the replacement or repayment time. In the case of burglary, photographs can be used for identification -- to prove your property belongs to you, if it is recovered.

Your personal property should all be marked with your driver's license number followed by the abbreviation of the state. But this alone will not provide you with all the protection you need to ensure the replacement or recovery of what you own.

On this page and the following pages are categories and room-by-room listings for you to list your possessions and their values. Use additional sheets to list additional items and collections.

Copy these pages and when complete, store them with your important papers. Keep a copy in a safety-deposit box, with a trusted friend, or with a relative.

Items that are likely to be taken in a burglary.

ANTIQUES & HEIRLOOMS

Item /Brand /Year Purchased /Serial Number/Estimated Value /Appraised

Books
China
Clocks
Crystal
Figurines
Furniture
Lamps
Linens
Plates
Silver service
Silverware
Other

COLLECTIBLES/ART

Item /Brand /Year Purchased /Serial Number /Estimated Value /Appraised

Antiques
Art
Paintings
Figurines
Other

COLLECTIONS

Item /Brand /Year Purchased /Serial Number /Cost-Appraisal

Coins
Compact Disks
Movies
Records
Stamps
Other

CLOTHING

Item /Brand /Year Purchased /Serial Number /Cost-Appraisal

Evening Wear
Furs
Suits
Tuxedos
Other

CRAFT GOODS

Item /Brand /Year Purchased /Serial Number /Cost-Appraisal

Supplies
Tools
Other

ELECTRONICS

Item /Brand /Year Purchased /Serial Number /Cost-Appraisal

Clocks
Clock Radio
Compact Disk Player
Computer(s)
Computer Peripherals
Computer Printers
Computer Software
Games
Radios
Record Players
Stereo Equipment
Tape Recorders
Telephone
Telephone answering mach.
Televisions
Video Camera
Video Recorders
DVD Player
Records, tapes and DVDs (use separate sheet)
Other

ELECTRONIC APPLIANCES

Item /Brand /Year Purchased /Serial Number /Cost-Appraisal

Clothes Iron
Coffee Maker
Curling Irons
Fan, ceiling
Fan, portable
Hair Dryers
Microwave Oven
Sewing Machines
Toaster Ovens
Vacuum
Other

JEWELRY

Item /Brand /Year Purchased /Serial Number /Cost-Appraisal

Bracelets
Brooches
Earrings
Necklaces
Rings
Watches
Other

MUSICAL INSTRUMENTS

Item /Brand /Year Purchased /Serial Number /Cost-Appraisal

Electronic Keyboards
Organs
Piano
Other

OFFICE EQUIPMENT

Item /Brand /Year Purchased /Serial Number /Cost-Appraisal

Adding Machine
Calculator
Typewriters
Other

PHOTOGRAPHIC EQUIPMENT

Item /Brand /Year Purchased /Serial Number /Cost-Appraisal

Camera
Other

SPORTING GEAR

Item /Brand /Year Purchased /Serial Number /Cost-Appraisal

Bicycles
Bowling
Diving
Fishing
Golf
Guns
Skis
Swimming
Tennis Rackets
Other

TOOLS

Item /Brand /Year Purchased /Serial Number /Cost-Appraisal

Drills
Hand tools
Lawn mower
Power tools
Saws
Welding Equipment
Other

The following is for the recording of property items that are not necessarily prone to theft, but may be taken. You should have a record in the event of fire or some other disaster that could destroy them.

Household Items

LIVING ROOM

Number of Articles /Article /Year Purchased /Cost-Appraisal

| Accessories |
| Air Conditioner |
| Books |
| Bookcases |
| Cabinets and contents |
| Carpet/rug |
| Chairs |
| Closet and Contents |

Number of Articles /Article /Year Purchased /Cost-Appraisal

| Couches |
| Curtains and shades |
| Desk |
| Fireplace equipment |
| Lamps |
| Tables |
| Wall Units |
| Other |

DINING ROOM

Number of Articles /Article /Year Purchased /Cost-Appraisal

| Accessories |
| Air Conditioner |
| Buffet |
| Cabinets and contents |
| Carpet |
| Chairs |
| Curtains and shades |
| Tables |
| Wall shelves |
| Other |

KITCHEN, LAUNDRY ROOM

Number of Articles /Article /Year Purchased /Cost-Appraisal

| Accessories |
| Books |
| Cabinets and contents |
| Closet and contents |
| Clothes Dryer |
| Cookers |
| Crockery |
| Cutlery |

KITCHEN, LAUNDRY ROOM (CONT')

Number of Articles /Article /Year Purchased /Cost-Appraisal

Dishes
Dishwasher
Freezer
Glassware
Ironing Board
Kitchen Utensils
Linens
Pots and Pans
Refrigerator
Silverware
Stove
Tables
Washer/Dryer
Other

BEDROOM 1, MASTER

Number of Articles /Article /Year Purchased /Cost-Appraisal

Accessories
Air conditioner
Bed
Bedding
Books
Bureaus and contents
Carpets
Chairs
Chests and contents
Closet contents
Curtains and Shades
Desk
Dresser and contents
Dressing Table
Lamps
Mattresses
Springs
Tables
Wall Shelves
Other

BEDROOM 2

Number of Articles /Article /Year Purchased /Cost-Appraisal

Accessories
Air conditioner
Bed
Bedding
Books
Bureaus and contents
Carpets

BEDROOM 2 (CONT')

Number of Articles /Article /Year Purchased /Cost-Appraisal

Chairs
Chests and contents
Closet contents
Curtains and Shades
Desk
Dresser and contents
Dressing table
Lamps
Mattresses
Springs
Tables
Wall shelves
Other

BEDROOM 3

Number of Articles /Article /Year Purchased /Cost-Appraisal

Accessories
Air conditioner
Bed
Bedding
Books
Bureaus and contents
Carpets
Chairs
Chests and contents
Closet contents
Curtains and thades
Desk
Dresser and contents
Dressing table
Lamps
Mattresses
Springs
Tables
Wall shelves
Other

BEDROOM 4

Number of Articles /Article /Year Purchased /Cost-Appraisal

Accessories
Air conditioner
Bed
Bedding
Books
Bureaus and contents
Carpets
Chairs

BEDROOM 4 (CONT')

Number of Articles /Article /Year Purchased /Cost-Appraisal

Dresser and contents
Chests and contents
Closet contents
Curtains and shades
Desk
Dressing table
Lamps
Mattresses
Springs
Tables
Wall Shelves
Other

FAMILY ROOM

Number of Articles /Article /Year Purchased /Cost-Appraisal

Accessories
Air conditioners
Books
Bookcases
Cabinets and contents
Card tables
Carpet
Chairs
Closet and contents
Couches
Curtains and shades
Desk
File cabinets
Fireplace equipment
Lamps
Tables
Wall shelves
Other

HALLWAY

Number of Articles /Article /Year Purchased /Cost-Appraisal

Accessories
Cabinets and contents
Carpet
Chairs
Closet contents
Curtains and shades
Lamps
Tables
Other

BATHROOM 1,

Number of Articles /Article /Year Purchased /Cost-Appraisal

Bathroom scale
Cabinets and contents
Chairs
Clothes hamper
Linens
Other

BATHROOM 2,

Number of Articles /Article /Year Purchased /Cost-Appraisal

Bathroom scale
Cabinets and contents
Chairs
Clothes hamper
Linens
Other

BASEMENT

Number of Articles /Article /Year Purchased /Cost-Appraisal

Accessories
Carpet
Chairs
Dehumidifier
Dryer
Heating unit
Luggage
Other equipment
Rugs
Tables
Trunk and contents
Washing machines
Workbench
Other

ATTIC

Number of Articles /Article /Year Purchased /Cost-Appraisal

Furniture
Luggage
Trunk and contents
Other

GARAGE

Number of Articles /Article /Year Purchased /Cost-Appraisal

Auto equipment
Garden tools
Lawn furniture
Lawn games
Other tools
Other

ADDITIONAL LISTINGS

Item /Brand /Year Purchased /Serial Number /Cost-Appraisal

SUSPICIOUS ACTIVITY / CRIME REPORT

Community WATCH

Was this a: *(check one)* ☐ CRIME   ☐ SUSPICIOUS ACTIVITY

Briefly describe what happened: _____

When did it happen? DATE: _____ TIME: _____

Where did it happen?
STREET: _____
ADDRESS: _____
NEAREST CROSS STREET: _____

SUSPECT DESCRIPTION

Sex: ☐ MALE   ☐ FEMALE

Age: _____ Height: _____ Weight: _____ Race: _____

Hair Color: _____ Mustache, beard or sideburns: _____

Glasses: _____ Color of eyes: _____ Complexion: _____

Tattoos, amputations, scars and/or other distinguishing marks: _____

Noticeable accents or special characteristics of speech: _____

CLOTHING

Shirt: _____ Coat: _____ Trousers: _____

Shoes: _____ Tie: _____ Hat: _____

Rings, Bracelets, Necklaces or Earrings: _____

WEAPON

Handgun: _____ Rifle: _____ Knife: _____ Club: _____ Other: _____

DESCRIPTION OF VEHICLE

Make: _____ Year: _____ Body Style: _____ Color: _____

License Number: _____ State: _____ (if unable to identify state, color of license): _____

Identifying dents, scratches, wheels, markings: _____

ANSWER THE FOLLOWING

Number of subjects: _____ What they said: _____

Direction of departure: _____

Name and addresses of other witnesses: _____

Your name: _____ Your phone: _____

Your address: _____

Community Watch Materials Available from Crime Prevention Resources

Over the past decade, Crime Prevention Resources has developed a wide array of tools to help you implement and maintain your Community Watch Program. Call us toll free at 1-800-867-0016 for further information. Ask about volume discounts.

No-Risk Guarantee

We are so sure that these materials will work for your community that we offer an unconditional money-back guarantee. If you are not completely satisfied, just return the product(s) and we will issue a complete refund or credit.

Community Watch Signs and Decals

The Sign that Stops Crime

The thief's greatest fear is that you will see him and identify him. Use this sign to reinforce his fear and make him think twice. Three different sizes to choose from. Ask about Custom Imprints!

Community Watch Decals

For Home

Teach citizens how to mark their property. Then put burglars on notice with these handy 3-inch by 5-inch decals.

For Business

Put this 3-inch by 5-inch decal on the front and back door of business establishments to warn criminals that they are being watched.

Community Watch Publications

The Block Captain's Handbook

Teach citizens how to take command of their neighborhoods and organize themselves into effective Community Watch organizations. Used by crime watch groups all across the USA during the annual National Night Out, this inexpensive handbook turns your recruitment and training of Block Captains into an efficient and effective process. Use it together with the video, "Community Policing: The Block Captain's Role" for a complete training package. [See next page for video details.]

The Citizen's Guide to Community Watch

To get the best participation from your citizens, give them a training tool that will help them seize the initiative. This handbook familiarizes readers with what a Community Watch is and isn't. The handbook also discusses the benefits gained from participation in the program as well as the responsibilities involved. Use it together with the video, "Community Policing: The Citizen's Role." [See next page for video details.]

The Community Watch Administration Manual, Third Edition

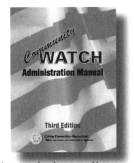

"I was so enthused by this book. It would make an excellent textbook for the crime prevention practitioner or criminal justice student." Sgt. Martin J. Jacobson, Training Coordinator for Stuart (FL) Police Department and Adjunct Professor with Palm Beach Criminal Justice Institute and Florida Crime Prevention Training Institute.

The Third Edition offers more helpful advice and more training tools than earlier editions.

Call 1-800-867-0016 for information about volume discounts.

Community and Neighborhood Watch Videos

BLUEPRINT FOR A SAFE COMMUNITY

Learn how to make your community a safer place to live and work. Crime statistics prove the effectiveness of Community Watch Programs. This program gives viewers many reasons to get involved. Great for service club meetings, block meetings and any other community gathering. 10 minutes. Catalog #V9202.

A LINE IN THE SAND: TAKING A STAND AGAINST CRIME

Don't use this video unless you're ready to sign up some volunteers for your program! Nominated for an Emmy Award, A Line in the Sand recreates two actual crimes to show the difference involved citizens can make in nabbing criminals. Highly motivational, this program can also help you attract business and community support for your program. 24 minutes. Catalog #V9501.

COMMUNITY POLICING: THE BLOCK CAPTAIN'S ROLE

Train a new Block Captain easily with this video, which shows how to start a new Community Watch block group. Also shows how to help neighbors overcome their fears of getting involved. Comes with a complimentary copy of The Block Captain's Handbook. 13 minutes. Catalog #V9603.

COMMUNITY POLICING: THE CITIZEN'S ROLE

What is suspicious activity? How do you report it? Will reporting really make any difference? This video teaches citizens that they are the eyes and ears of law enforcement. Working together through an effective Community Watch Program, citizens really can make a difference. Comes with a complimentary copy of the Citizen's Guide to Community Watch. 14 minutes. Catalog #V9602.

BLUEPRINT FOR HOME SECURITY

Preventing home burglary is the number one reason why citizens start Community Watch Programs. This program shows how to "target harden" a residence and what to do when leaving home. Comes with a complimentary copy of the Home Security Survey. 15 minutes. Catalog #V9201.

RURAL CRIME PREVENTION

Applies Community Watch concepts to the special needs of rural citizens. How to secure your boundaries more effectively, how to reduce theft, vandalism, rustling and other crimes of opportunity. How to work effectively with neighbors and law enforcement. 27 minutes. Catalog #V0103.

CONDITIION RED - PREPARED FOR DISASTER

This video tells you what you need to do to be better prepared for a terrorist attack and other disasters. Provides an overview of family emergency planning and how to stay safe in your home. Finally, the program discusses the power of neighbors working together through Community Watch Programs. 24 minutes. Catalog #V0304.

See www.crimeprevent.com or call 1-800-867-0016 for a complete list of our crime prevention videos.